175285

745.67
Got   Göttingen. Nieder-
          sächsische...

The Göttingen
model book

THE GÖTTINGEN MODEL BOOK

THE GÖTTINGEN MODEL BOOK

A FACSIMILE EDITION AND TRANSLATIONS OF A

FIFTEENTH-CENTURY ILLUMINATORS' MANUAL

EDITED, WITH COMMENTARY BY HELLMUT LEHMANN-HAUPT

BASED IN PART ON THE STUDIES OF THE LATE DR. EDMUND WILL

UNIVERSITY OF MISSOURI PRESS, COLUMBIA

ISBN 0–8262–0261–6   All rights reserved
Library of Congress Catalog Card Number 78–62289

Copyright © 1972 by The Curators of the University of Missouri
University of Missouri Press, Columbia, Missouri 65211

Second Printing, Revised, 1978
Printed and bound in the United States of America

The page of the Berlin Model Book is reproduced by permission of the Staatliche Museen Preussischer Kulturbesitz, Berlin.

The facsimile of the Göttingen Model Book is reproduced by permission of the Niedersächsische Staats- und Universitätsbibliothek, Göttingen.

Figure 1 is reproduced by permission of the Niedersächsische Staats- und Universitätsbibliothek, Göttingen.

Figures 2, 3, 4, 5, and 6 are reproduced by permission of the Stadt- und Universitäts-Bibliothek, Frankfurt am Main.

Figures 7, 8, 13, 14, and 15 are reproduced by permission of the Stadtarchiv der Stadt Mainz and the Stadtbibliothek der Stadt Mainz.

Figures 9 and 10 are reproduced by permission of the Bibliothèque Nationale, Paris.

Figures 11 and 12 are reproduced by permission of the Universitätsbibliothek, Giessen.

Figure 16 is reproduced by permission of Foto Marburg, Marburg/Lahn.

Figure 17 is reproduced by permission of the Library of Congress, Washington, D.C.

TO INGEBORG

CONTENTS

ACKNOWLEDGMENTS, 9

INTRODUCTION, 11

MODEL BOOK FACSIMILE, 20

MODERN GERMAN TRANSLATION, 33

ENGLISH TRANSLATION, 57

WORKS INFLUENCED BY THE MODEL BOOK, 81

POSTSCRIPT, 101

The list of those who gave me valued aid in the preparation of this study of the Göttingen Model Book is long. In addition to the librarians and curators who made it possible for me to examine the Göttingen Model Book and the many volumes influenced by it, there were others who graciously gave me assistance of varied and specialized kinds.

The late Dr. Edmund Will, formerly of the staff of the Göttingen Library, devoted much time to a detailed study of the Göttingen Model Book, but he interrupted his work—for reasons unknown to me—a good while before his death several years ago. He left behind a sizable apparatus of transcriptions, glossaries, comparative notes, and materials of like nature in preparation of what promised to be a most ambitious publication. In addition to exhaustive philological and linguistic study of the text he evidently planned detailed comparisons of the color recipes with those in other contemporary artists' manuals, and also thoroughgoing studies of the samples of illumination, in the perspectives of art history. The work he planned clearly exceeded the capacities of a single individual, and it is not really surprising that he interrupted his labors. I am most grateful to have this opportunity to acknowledge my debt to him, for I consider his work to be the basis of mine.

Dr. Wilhelm Grunwald, the director of the Göttingen Library, Mr. Helmut Vogt, acting director, and Dr. Klaus Haenel, the chief of its Manuscript Division, made available for my study certain portions of the Will papers by sending them on International Interlibrary Loan to the University of Missouri in Columbia. For generous assistance in this and other matters I am deeply grateful to these three gentlemen.

I realized very early in my study of these materials that it would not be possible for a single individual to bring to fruition Dr. Will's ambitious plans. I therefore limited my work to what I hope will be recognized as a sensible first step, a basis on which future work can be built in due time, as specialists in various facets of the book bring their learning to bear on it.

I am greatly indebted to Mrs. Elgin van Treeck (née Vaassen). In the preparation of her Würzburg doctoral dissertation on the Giant Bible of Würzburg, a masterpiece of fifteenth-century Mainz illumination, she found a rewarding group of manuscripts and early printed books that had been illuminated according to the instructions and samples of the Göttingen Model Book. Mrs. van Treeck's list provided the basis for the chapter in this book entitled "Works Influenced by the Model Book."

The American Council of Learned Societies generously gave me a travel grant that enabled me, in the summer of 1968, to examine at first hand the many books illuminated according to the instructions of the Göttingen Model Book. The Research Council of the University of Missouri aided the physical preparation of the manuscript with a grant under which Mrs. Marcia Collins accomplished a difficult assignment of typing.

Professor H. Roosen-Runge of the Art Department of Würzburg University sponsored Mrs. van Treeck's dissertation. I am deeply grateful to him for his scholarly assistance in the preparation of this publication. Professors Joachim Kirchner of Munich and Werner Bischoff of Planegg near Munich kindly suggested the proper reading of the inscription in the Butzbach Bible, which I discuss briefly in its relationship to the Göttingen Model Book. Professor Robert J. Rowland, Department of Classical Languages of the University of Missouri, Columbia, translated one of these inscriptions and a Latin passage elsewhere into good modern English.

In addition to Dr. Haenel, the following librarians were most helpful in making available their treasures and in arranging for photographs: Bibliotheksoberrat Dr. Schüling, Giessen University Library; Dr. Gerhardt Powitz, chief of the Manuscript Department of the Frankfurt Municipal and University Library; in Mainz, Dr. Elizabeth Geck of the Gutenberg Museum, Dr. Ella Darapski of the Municipal Archives, and Dr. Christian Gündel, the curator of the Dom Museum; in Paris, the late Mlle Erwana Brim, conservateur, chef du service de la Réserve, and Mlle Marie-Henriette Besnier, conservateur à la Réserve; in Washington, Mr. Frederick R. Goff, chief of the Rare Book Division in the Library of Congress. Dr. Fedja Anzelewski of the Berlin Kupferstichkabinett generously supplied information on the Berlin Model Book.

The dedication of this work to my wife Ingeborg is in grateful acknowledgment of her substantial and ever-patient assistance in many phases of its preparation.

H. L.-H., Columbia, Missouri, January 1971, June 1978

I first saw the Göttingen Model Book in the spring of 1961. I had known of its existence for some time, but I had never had the opportunity to examine it. There was a special reason why I was eager to see the manuscript, which had remained unpublished—actually unknown to all but a very few scholars.[1] That spring I had traveled to Germany, mainly to investigate a number of tantalizing questions raised by the amazing discovery that the Giant Bible of Mainz—a magnificent manuscript written in two large volumes on the purest vellum, which Lessing Rosenwald had given to the Library of Congress[2]—had marginal miniatures very closely associated with a set of early engraved playing cards. Many little flowers, deer, bears, lions and "wild men," and hairy monsters in fantastic costumes were found to be identical in size and design in the margins of the Bible with the copper engravings made by the so-called Master of the Playing Cards, the earliest European copper engraver to practice intaglio engraving. The presence in libraries in Mainz and elsewhere in Germany—and for that matter in the United States—of other Mainz manuscripts and incunabula with many "playing card" motifs suggested very strongly that there had been a common source.[3] It seemed virtually inescapable to assume that a model book of some kind must have existed in Mainz around the middle of the fifteenth century, and that it had inspired both illuminators and the earliest of all engravers. Was the manuscript in Göttingen perhaps the lost model book?

It was with considerable curiosity and anticipation that I went to Göttingen and asked to see the little treasure. Little, certainly, it is: a slight volume measuring c. 15.8 × 10.5 cm., with only 22 pages of text and illumination. A hasty first perusal revealed all sorts of patterns for illuminated decoration, but no figures, no little men, birds, beasts, or flowers. My initial disappointment quickly gave way, however, to joyful elation. Never, in well over forty years spent in the study of books and manu-scripts, had I seen any work to compare with this small gem. The light vellum pages of the perfectly preserved little volume are covered with an easily legible German cursive script, written in ink of various shades of brown, interspersed with sparklingly fresh models for ornamental borders. Each of the models shows carefully the closely integrated progressive stages of execution, and small circles with shiny specks of gold leaf demonstrate how to make various backgrounds for initial letters, which stand out

1. My book, *Gutenberg and the Master of the Playing Cards* (New Haven, Yale University Press, 1966), gives a short description on pages 21 and 22, and in figures 13 and 14 (in color).

2. See Dorothy Miner, *The Giant Bible of Mainz, 500th Anniversary* (Washington, D.C., 1952).

3. See Lehmann-Haupt, *op. cit.*, pp. 16, 23, 42 ff., 71.

from among the lines of writing like jeweled sprays and circles. At the end are three pages without text that contain colored patterns to show how to fill the stems of illuminated letters and some large foliage.

Twice again, in 1968 and 1969, did I make the pilgrimage to the Göttingen Library, the "Niedersächsische Staats- und Universitäts Bibliothek," as it is officially known. The Göttingen Model Book was to be seen also in New York early in 1968, when it was one of the highlights of the Grolier Club's exhibition held in observance of the five-hundredth anniversary of the death of Johann Gutenberg. Each time, during and after intensive study of the text and its close relationship with most of the illuminations, I fell under the spell of the unique beauty and charm of this manuscript.

Shortly after the first publication of *The Göttingen Model Book* I learned that a manuscript very similar to the Göttingen Model Book existed in Berlin. I will discuss the Berlin Model Book more fully on pages 17–18.

Enthusiastic response to an artistic creation may be a personal matter, but there are solid, objective reasons why the GMB (as I shall term it hereafter) and the Berlin Model Book are of unique significance and importance.

There are four main points that, to the best of my knowledge, prove that the two model books embody features and characteristics not found in any other model book.

1. The model books are exclusively concerned with the ornamental embellishment of margins and initial letters of manuscripts and books; they have no human figures, animals, or other miscellaneous elements.
2. To the best of my knowledge these are the only model books to contain both verbal instructions and pictorial models in color that explain the production of decorative illumination in a closely integrated sequence of successive steps.
3. They are the only model books to contain both pictorial models and detailed verbal explanations for their production and also specific practical instructions for the preparation and application of the various colors used in book illumination.[4]
4. There is no other medieval model book in existence that can be identified, clearly and without ambiguities, as the direct source of the illumination of an entire group of manuscripts and early printed books.

Certainly, that initial pilgrimage to Göttingen was most generously rewarding to me.

Certain explanations and qualifications are in order here. They will, however, serve only to strengthen the validity of the four points set out above.

The best modern study of model books is R. W. Scheller's *A Survey of Medieval Model Books* (Harlem, 1963). Scheller does not mention GMB in this first edition of his survey, but he will in the forthcoming second edition. The model books described in the first edition contain mainly human figures, but there are also animals, birds,

4. Verbal instructions alone are, of course, in existence. See *An Anonymous Fourteenth-Century Treatise, DE ARTE ILLUMINANDI, the Technique of Manuscript Illumination, translated from the Latin of Naples MS. XII E. 27,* translated by Daniel Varney Thompson, Jr., and George Heard Hamilton (New Haven, 1933); Cennino d'Andrea Cennini, *The Craftsman's Handbook. The Italian "Il Libro dell'arte,"* trans. by Daniel V. Thompson, Jr. (New York, 1954); Julius v. Schlosser, "Zur Kenntnis d. Künstl. Überlieferung im späten Ma.," in *Jahrbuch d. Kunsthistorischen Sammlungen d. Allerhöchsten Kaiserhauses,* XXII (1902), pp. 279 ff.; Emil Ploss, "Studien z. d. deutschen Maler- und Färberbüchern des Mittelalters" (doctoral thesis, Munich, 1952). In typescript only. Ploss does not know GMB, but is well informed on the surviving manuscripts in general.

architectural details, alphabets, and miscellaneous designs, including patterns for manuscript decorations. It should be noted that in the Giovanni de' Grassi sketch book (Scheller No. 21) some foliage resembles the Göttingen and Berlin model books so closely that de' Grassi's work must surely be a direct ancestor of these books. Through what channels of transmittal its characteristics reappear in these two model books is impossible to trace at this point.

Scheller mentions connections between some of the model books and certain illuminated manuscripts. The de' Grassi model book and some of the others listed are definitely connected by various resemblances to certain illuminated manuscripts. Scheller does not explain the nature of their relation in detail, whether it is mainly iconographic or stylistic, or both. His observations, however, open an entire field for further intensive studies and comparisons that would trace and assess the nature of these connections precisely. From the data given by Scheller it seems doubtful that one would find any connections as direct and close as those between the Göttingen and Berlin model books and the manuscripts and early printed books described in this work. There is certainly no case known at the present time of such direct connection between a model book and an entire group of volumes illuminated according to its instructions.

At this point I might mention my interesting experience with the thirteenth-century *Bestiary* (Scheller No. 13), in the possession of Philip Hofer. This codex, upon examination, proved to be a model book (see Samuel A. Ives and Hellmut Lehmann-Haupt, *An English 13th Century Bestiary* [New York, H. P. Kraus, 1942]). It contained the text for a bestiary, with spaces left for illustrations and, on a group of separate pages, the illustrations. The outlines of all the miniatures in this section had been pin-pricked, obviously for the purpose of transferring these designs as silhouettes onto the pages of bestiary manuscripts that were presumably prepared in an early secular workshop that made multiple copies for sale. We were very curious whether the publication of this model book would reveal any surviving bestiaries that had been copied from the Hofer Codex. In the nearly thirty years since its publication not a single example has come to light. This is one of the reasons why the discovery of the two model books, with their large group of dependent monuments, is so significant.

One further point should be elucidated. I have stated, as their second feature of uniqueness, that the Göttingen and Berlin model books are the only model books known that describe the production of decorative illumination in a closely integrated sequence of successive steps. Several of the model books described by Scheller show in their illustrations underlying designs in lead or silverpoint that have been retraced, usually with a pen. Many of the retracings can be identified as later efforts to preserve the fading original drawings. It is obvious that these overlays have nothing to do with the separate step-by-step designs in GMB.

DESCRIPTION OF THE GÖTTINGEN MODEL BOOK

GMB is neither a large nor a thick volume. Actually, it is a single signature of 11 vellum folios, each measuring c. 15.8 × 10.5 cm., with minor variations from page to page. Folios 1 and 11, 2 and 10, and 3 and 9 are conjugates. Folios 4 and 5 are on stubs inserted from the left, and folios 6, 7, and 8 are on stubs inserted from the right. The arrangement of the leaves is best understood from the following diagram:

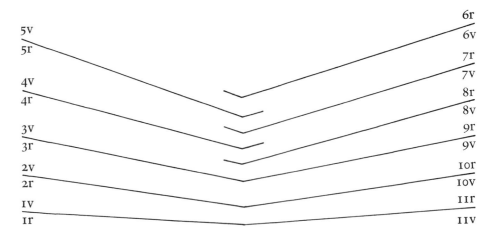

The rectos of all folios from 1 to 11 bear arabic numerals in pencil that are of comparatively recent origin—nineteenth or twentieth century.

The vellum leaves are bound in an unpretentious and inconspicuous cover of blue cardboard, reinforced along the spine with a strip of bluish-gray cloth that is becoming detached in spots. In the lower left corner of the front cover is a small pasted-on label of slightly browned paper with the 2-line inscription, "Cod. Ms. / Uffenb. 51." Inside the front cover, in the upper left corner, is the 2-line pencil notation, "Cod. Uffenb. 51 / (963)." Below, center, pasted in, is the description of the codex from the following printed catalog: *Verzeichnis der Handschriften im Preussischen Staate I. Hannover 3. Göttingen 3*, Berlin, A. Barth, 1894. (2d title page:) *Hannover. / Die Handschriften in Göttingen.* (3d title page:) *Universitäts-Bibliothek / Nachlässe von Gelehrten, Orientalische / Handschriften / Handschriften im Besitz von Instituten / und Behörden / . . .* Berlin, A. Barth, 1894.[5]

5. An English analysis of the contents will be found on pp. 16 and 17.

Pasted in at the front of the manuscript is a printed form with rules for users and handwritten entries by the various readers who have studied the manuscript.

The manuscript is kept in a slightly larger portfolio made of an old-fashioned decorative paper, with a blue strip of cloth along the spine and four small cloth corners. There is a printed label of gray paper, pasted onto the front cover of the portfolio, with the 4-line inscription, "Anleitung / zum Ornamentmalen / auf Pergament / 15. Jh." The inside of the back cover of the portfolio has three flaps under which the manuscript is fitted.

On the lower left corner of the front cover of the portfolio is pasted a handwritten label similar to the one on the front cover of the binding, which has the same 2-line inscription, "Cod. Ms. / Uffenb. 51." On folio 1r of the codex (see the facsimile) is an old stamp, of which two lines are legible: DONAT. / UFFENBACH; the stamp is repeated on folio 1v, with portions of another line above and the date 1769 below.

PROVENANCE

The stamp on folios 1r and 1v indicates that GMB was part of the bequest of the Frankfurt patrician Johann Friedrich Armand von Uffenbach (1687–1769).[6] He shared a passion for books with his more famous bibliophile brother Zacharias Konrad von Uffenbach (1683–1734),[7] whom he accompanied on many learned expeditions. The former's book collection centered on mathematics, physics, technology, military science, and iconographic and topographic works. Johann Friedrich A. von Uffenbach also owned instruments, models, and—a significant clue to his interest in the early history of graphic tradition—drawings and copper engravings. On July 28, 1736, Uffenbach declared in an official document that after his death his library and instruments, with all subsequent additions, should go to the *Georgia Augusta* (the Göttingen University Library). Characteristically, the document specified that the materials should be housed in separate repositories for public, permanent use. It was not until thirty-three years later, after Uffenbach's death in 1769, that the gift was consummated.

When and how GMB was acquired by Uffenbach is not known today. Nor is it possible to say whether archival research can ever answer the question.[8]

THE TEXT

The manuscript of GMB begins inconspicuously enough with a single line heading *Laupp Werk* (Foliage), and then follows this sequence:

6. The following data were gathered from *Geschichte der Göttinger Universitäts-Bibliothek*, Karl Julius Hartmann and Hans Füchsel, eds. (Göttingen, Vandenhoeck & Rupprecht, 1937). See also *Allgemeine Deutsche Biographie*, vol. 39 (1895), pp. 133–34.

7. See G. A. E. Bogeng, *Die grossen Bibliophilen* (Leipzig, E. A. Seemann, 1922).

8. The published catalog of the Göttingen mss. records the Model Book in the list of the Uffenbach donations under No. 51, without any indication of previous owners or other provenance.

F.1r–4r. These seven pages offer detailed instructions and illustrations, in closely connected, progressive stages, on how to design and illuminate three different kinds of acanthus leaf decorations, each of the same simple basic design, each with two corresponding colors. F.1r–2v show an acanthus leaf in rose color with a green reverse in six successive illustrations. F.2v–3r show, in only five stages, the design of the leaf in minium and purple. F.3v–4r, again in only five stages, show a leaf in blue and the so-called aurum musicum, with the fifth illustration of the third acanthus leaf occupying only the top of f.4r.

F.4r. The balance of this page, without any heading, has instructions on how to prepare the "assis" or great gold ground.

F.4v–6v. On f.4v begins material under a 2-line heading, *Wie Du alle varbe temperieren / und riben sullent* (How you shall temper all colors and grind them), that occupies most of the next five pages. The colors are treated on the pages from f.4v to f.6r in the following order: F.4v, blue, aurum musicum, dark brown or dark red (continued to f.5r); f.5r, light rose, lead white and lead yellow, green (continued to 5v). The balance of f.5v treats dark green and minium. F.6r begins with instructions on smoke black and purple, then offers a note on how to shade and heighten the various colors. Without heading, instructions follow on how to apply certain colors, how to grind and temper them, when to use the brush and when the pen, how to let colors dry well before new applications, and how to moisten them.

F.6v–9v. Within line 27 on f.6v appears a new heading without underlining: Vier Feldung dar usz gan daz / merteyl aller feldung (Four checkered backgrounds, from which come the majority of all backgrounds). This topic occupies the balance of f.6v and continues part way through f.9v in the following sequence: F.7r. General instructions for the preparation of the backgrounds. Instructions for the first of the four, simply designated as chessboard or checkered background, begin on line 13 of this page, and the first steps are illustrated by a pair of circles. The instructions continue through f.7v to f.8r, illustrated on f.7v by two pairs of small circles and on f.8r with another two pairs to show, closely coordinated, the construction of the first checkered background. There follows, beginning with line 15 on f.8r, a simple sentence heading: Dysz ist die ander feldung (This is the second checkered background). This instruction continues to f.8v, which it occupies to the bottom. Only three pairs of circles illustrate these points. F.9r has a separate 1-line heading: *Die dritte Feldung* (The Third Checkered Background). The description takes up the balance of this page, with three pairs of illustrative circles. F.9v begins with a separate 1-line heading: *Die vierde Feldung* (The Fourth Checkered Background). The description occupies only the first five lines and shows only one pair of circles.

F.9v–10r. The balance of f.9v, with the change indicated abruptly and with but a 2-line marginal heading, *Nota Aurum musicum*, offers a precisely detailed and specific instruction on how to prepare aurum musicum, which continues through f.10r and concludes the text.

F.10v–11v. The final three pages are filled with models for the illumination of initial letters and decorations for the margins. Curiously enough, these three pages are without any textual explanation whatsoever. F.10v has on the upper half of the page three models showing how to fill the stems of rather large initial letters. It is important to understand that they do not represent a single letter, M for instance, but are three separate, independent units. On the lower half of the page is a stylized flower bud or blossom of fairly large size. F.11r displays in monumental fashion a single large acanthus border in purple and minium, wound around a staff. F.11v, the last leaf of the manuscript, has on the left a long acanthus border in green and red, drawn on approximately the same scale as the leaves described earlier in the Model Book. On the right is a shorter leafy scroll in blue and aurum musicum, which is approximately of the same size as the scroll on f.11r.

It might be observed at this point that the manuscript has a curiously casual composition. Headings of important divisions are not consistently displayed on separate, underscored lines, but are sometimes tucked away in the text or displayed as marginal notations. There is frequent use of paragraph marks and larger initial letters, as the reader can best observe by an inspection of the facsimile itself.

DESCRIPTION OF THE BERLIN MODEL BOOK

The Berlin Model Book is currently in the possession of the Print Room (Kupferstichkabinett) of the Staatliche Museen Preussischer Kulturbesitz in Berlin. Dr. Fedja Anzelewski of the Print Room was kind enough to supply a description of the Berlin Model Book (which I have translated below) and a transcription of the first line of text on each folio:

The manuscript 78 A 22 contains today 18 vellum leaves measuring 158 by 104 millimeters, but originally it had 24 leaves (see below). These 24 leaves are arranged in two signatures, each of 6 double leaves, and they were originally counted by the leaves in each signature. In the first signature only the number 6 is preserved, of the second all figure numbers are still legible. After these leaves there are again 6 paper leaves with color recipes in a sixteenth-century hand, sewed into the same original vellum cover.

Folio 1r: lapp werk. Das lapp soll man zu dem ersten / mit aim bly oder mit aim Sthöfft / entwerffen / also hie stet

There follows a leaf of foliage drawn in line; this foliage deviates in its form from

Berlin Model Book, Page 5r.

the one in GMB. Illustrating this first section of the text, which is in folios 1r–4r, the little manuscript contains 15 drawings.

Folios 4v–5r and 5v–6r each have 5 drawings with the foliage in blue and red and also in blue and gold.

Folio 6v–7r: Dass assis

Folio 7r–8r: von dem golt grunt und sime gebresten

Folio 8r–11: Wie ir alle varwen temperierent und ribent (with color samples for each color)

Folio 11v–12r: Wie man alle varwen schettewen soll

Folio 12r–12v: Dis sint die doten varwen

Folio 13r–18v: Vier feldunge dar us dz mertteil alle fendung us gan (with 26 drawings, some of them different from the Göttingen Model Book).

Missing are the illustrations that are to be found in the Göttingen folios 10v–11v. They may have been on the three leaves that were cut out at the end of the second signature. Also missing is a leaf in the first signature between folios 8 and 9 of the current pagination. Whether this means that both text and illustrations were lost cannot be decided since neither ink nor color particles are preserved on the remaining strips.

The Berlin manuscript is the subject of a dissertation, soon to be completed, by Ms. Gisela Höhle. Ms. Höhle will edit the text of the Berlin Model Book and will consider it in connection with Mainz book illustrations, particularly in Gutenberg's 42-line Bible.

THE POSITION OF THE GÖTTINGEN AND BERLIN MODEL BOOKS IN ART HISTORY

The Göttingen and Berlin model books are of high quality. They present us with a strongly convincing combination of taste and technical excellence. To be sure, the acanthus leaves, compared with some of the glories of, for instance, Austrian illumination, or of the Giant Bible of Mainz, are perhaps a trifle on the robust side. But, as is pointed out in the discussion of the model books and their followers, these models are of extraordinary flexibility and allow almost infinite variation in use. Moreover, the models for the filling of the stems of the initial letters and, above all, for the four checkered backgrounds, are as finely worked as one could desire—a sheer delight. At the same time, these two model books are assuredly not original. Any student who knows late medieval book illumination will be able to point to connections with examples from almost anywhere in Europe.

Certainly one can, with research, trace the more remote as well as the more immediate ancestors of the motifs of these model books. I did not feel that an exhaustive search for their antecedents was essential to this edition, and I have therefore made no attempt to trace these connections. Study of the model books and their ancestry and descendants can afford fascinating and rewarding research for students of illumination.

No, the Göttingen and Berlin model books are not original, they are not experimental, nor do they represent an attempt to be progressive. They record current practice, decidedly, and herein resides their very virtue. They tell us what techniques were practiced in Mainz around the middle of the century, and they tell us most explicitly how they were applied. This information is of inestimable value to present-day scholars, for which all students should be grateful.

One more thought. It might well be wondered why these books made their appearance so relatively late in the development of illumination. To be sure, the middle of the fifteenth century was a time of great book-making activity in Mainz: The 42-line Bible and perhaps other early books were being set; such splendid codices as the Giant Bible of Mainz were being written and illuminated. It is only in recent years that scholars have become aware of the virtuosity and variety of manuscript illumination that was being done at that period in Mainz.[9] Last, but certainly not least, the Master of the Playing Cards may have been making his first engravings at about that time in Mainz.

Still, there is no reason to assume that all this activity started suddenly around the year 1450. It undoubtedly resulted from a long tradition that began earlier in the century. As scholars work back toward the sources of this great flowering of book art, they will undoubtedly enrich our knowledge of its predecessors. Yet, the model books made their appearance relatively late. Could it be that their production was prompted by the fear that the traditional craft of book illumination was threatened by printing, that the practitioners of the art somehow felt compelled to go on record, to codify their practices, protect them against extinction? The same phenomenon occurred in the field of formal book writing. It is only from the fifteenth century on that we begin to see, slowly at first, and then with increasing frequency, the appearance of written and then printed writing manuals—the writing masters' copybooks that played such an important part in the Renaissance.[10] Also, the geometric construction of letters, mainly the Roman capitals, arose likewise during the later fifteenth and the early sixteenth century.[11] Perhaps we do owe the appearance of the Göttingen and Berlin model books in part to apprehension and fear; perhaps it was intended as an insurance against oblivion.

9. See Elgin Vaassen, "Die Werkstatt der Mainzer Riesenbibel in Würzburg (Mp. th. f. m.11) und ihr Umkreis" (Würzburg dissertation not yet published).

10. See Baltimore Museum of Art, *Two Thousand Years of Calligraphy* (Baltimore, 1965).

11. See Millard Meiss, *Andrea Mantegna as Illuminator* (New York, Columbia University Press, 1957).

MODEL BOOK FACSIMILE

THE FOLLOWING FACSIMILE IS IN THE EXACT SIZE OF THE ORIGINAL

Daz lauws sal ma zu de ersten mit eim bly od
mit eim stifft entwerffe dar nach sal man
daz lauws uß rißen miz eime falben vnd miz
vast dunce hinten od mir dune schwarczen
dar nach sal man daz lauws bruniere mit eim
zan Iz die varbe glat dar uff lege werden
mir vast dar nach sal ma es an streichen
mir de varben ein sijt echt vnd die and
sijt lind odre leg mit eim hensel stro
liechte roscl vnd grun also berd grun odn
schisteczgrun Die zelbo varben gehoren
zamen eim liechte roscl vnd den twnslach
grun also hie odr ein grun vnd den twin
flach liechte roscl also du e wiler zol

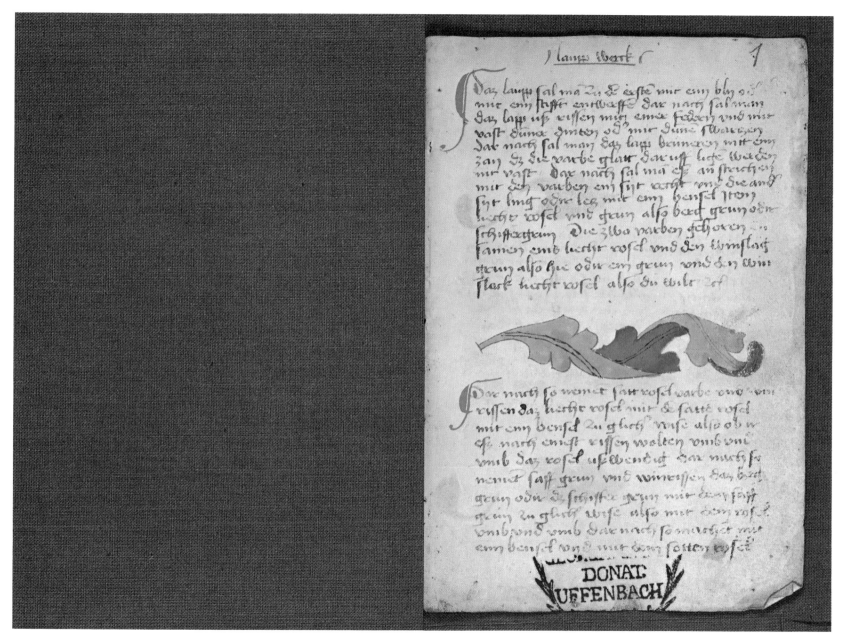

Dar nach so nemet satt roscl varbe vnd vm
reissen daz liechte roscl mit de satte roscl
mit eim bensel zu glich wise also ob ir
es nach einst reissen wolten vmb vnd
vmb daz roscl uswendig dar nach so
nemet saft grun vnd winreissen daz berd
grun odn de schiste grun mir deim saft
grun zu glich wise also mir deim roscl
vmb vnd vmb dar nach so mdechet mit
eim bensel vnd mit dem satten roscl

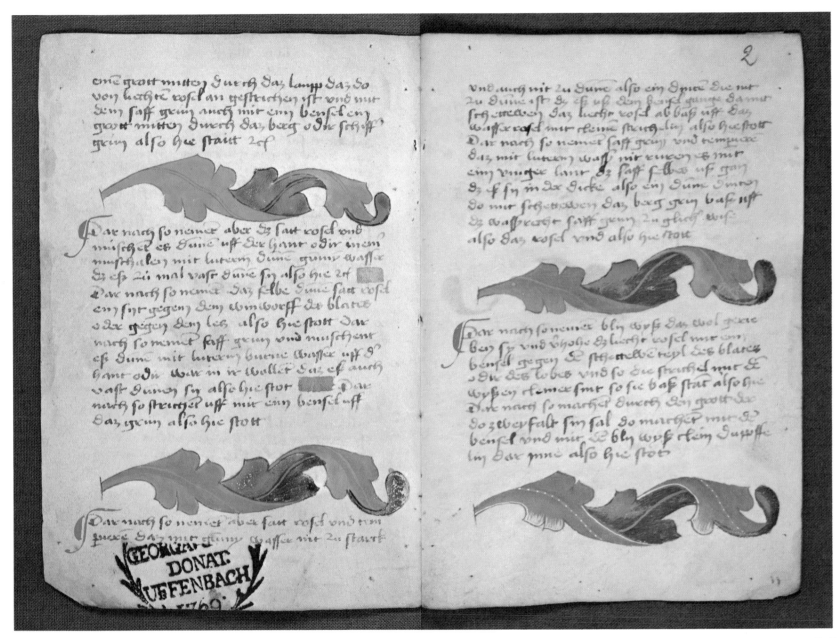

ene gtrott mitten durch das lanp das so
von liechte rosel an gestrichen ist vnd mit
dem safft grun auch mit ein bensel ein
gtrott mitten durch das berg oder schefft
grun also hie statt rot

Dar nach so nemet aber Es satt rosel vnd
mischet es dune uff der hant odir inem
muschalen mit lutern dune grun wasser
des zu mal vast dune sy also hie rot

Dar nach so nemet das selbe dune satt rosel
ein syt gegen dem ebmwbosff des blattes
oder gegen dem les also hie stott dar
nach so nemet safft grun vnd muschent
es dune mit lutern burne wasser uff der
hant odir war in ir wollet das es auch
vast dune sy also hie stot   Dar
nach so stertzet uff mit ein bensel uff
das grun also hie stott

Dar nach so nemet aber satt rosel vnd nem
grune das mit gleine wasser nit zu starck

vnd auch nit zu dune also ein spies die nit
zu dune ist des es uff den berg grune da mit
schetrellben das liecht rosel ab bass uff das
wasse rosel mit gleine sterchlin also hie stott
Dar nach so nemet safft grun vnd tempere
das mit lutern wasse mit einem es mit
ein vingerr lanr das safft selbes uff gan
das es sy in der dicke also ein dune tmen
do mit schetrellben das berg grun bass uff
das wasse recht safft grun zu gleich weis
also das rosel vnd also hie stott

Dar nach so nemet bly weiss das wol grire
bay sy vnd wholie Es liecht rosel mit ein
bensel gegen Es schetrellben tepl des blates
oder des leibes vnd so die sterchel mit Es
weysen glenee syr so sie bass stat also hie
Dar nach so machet durch den grott der
do zwerfalt sy sal do machet mit der
bensel vnd mit Es bly weiss elein stressle
bin dar unne also hie stot

Dar nach so machet m[it] der grenn auch in den
grott duffel vnd so nemet vol gerieben bly
gel getempriret mit grüm[e] dz fl[ein] dz uff
dem bensel gange Dz bly gel sal sin mit dem
rotten bly gel sunder dz grein vor gel
daz ist besser uff grein dz ist dz beste.
Dar nach so erhohent dz grein lou[b] uff
Die andern syt gegen der greuen schettlung
mit bly gel zu glich[e] wise also dz woll
mit dem bly uff also hie mit dem
bly gel also hie stott rol

Spreuge vnd hint die zwo farben
gehorch zu same an dem lou[b] wercke eins
recht vnd die andern syt linckt vnd
sullet dz loub vor hin entdecken mit
dem bly Dar nach rissen mit einer fed
dem vnd dar nach mit der mynge oder
mit grüne varbe anstreichen entz mynge
oder grüne vnd den vmb slag grüne oder
mynge we[r] wollet also hie stott

Dar nach neme rosel vnd grenn streichet die
mynge vnd die grüne varbe bede vmb vnd
vmb mit einem bensel vnd machet ein selber
falage grott dar durch mitten m[it] der lou[b]
also dan hie stott

Dar nach so nemet ab dz schtt rosel vnd
machet es vast dunn mit lautem grüme
wasse[r] zu glich[e] wise Also zu den liechten
rosel also da vornan stott vnd streichent die
bede varbe damit an vnd schtterbe sie Also hie

Dar nach so nemet ab satt rosel vnd schatte
wen es bas Also da vornan stott mit dem
liechten rosel vnd also hie stott

Dar nach so erhohet dz grüne mit bly uff vnd die
mynge mit bly gel erhohet also hie stott

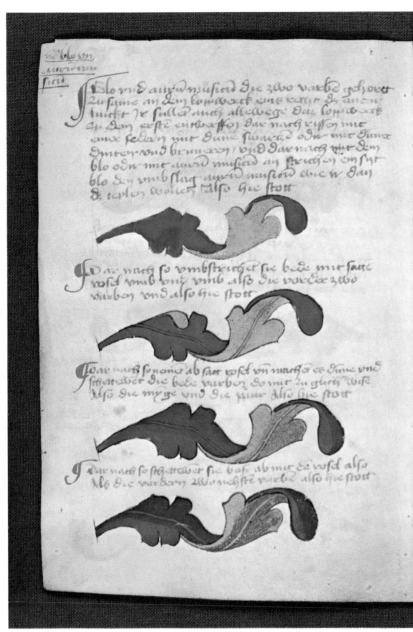

[3v]

[4r]

Wie du alle varbe temperest
von vliben sullent etc

Blo sullet ir mit rieben es sy dan gar grob ist
es grob so ribe es uff eyn erbesten das wirt
glatt sy oder uff eyn glase oder uff eyn rirbe
melstein also / wenne ir blo wilt legen es mit ...
lange uber nacht oder ein stuck oder zwo und
ribent es dan uff ein steyn an die lange mit eyer
clare die nach so flosse er recht wol mit lange
oder mit lutern glass und
lont es dan trucken uff ein bappier oder histen
eyn trucken geschirre so es ... und schon und
trucken ab geflossen hant und das so nement lut
gumy arabisch wasser do mit temperen ir es gerne
gumy arabisch wasser do mit es gerne
uff die seiden gange das gumy wasser sal lut sy
uff die seiden gange das gumy wasser sal lut sy
es es weiche zu dicke nach zu dunne sy und weche
es weiche zu dicke nach zu dunne sy Also es es wol habe
zu starck oder zu kranck sy Also es es wol habe
und auch nit zu glantz sy Das blo sal temperirt sy
das es gern uffe der seiden gange und uffe dem
bensel und sol es nit gern die uff gan so nement
eyn wenig zugker daran do var ... gern uff wol wol

Nuw mu...
Nuw mu... Das sullet ir mit wasser ... ir sullet
es triben mit lutern biern klass und sullet
es dan temperen mit lutern gumy Also das blo
an das zo der ir sullet es aber vor flossen mit
lutern biern klass und dar nach temperen als
vor geschriben ster nit zu starck und auch nit
zu kranck etc / nu sar brun oder nu sar rosel

Nu sar brun oder nu sar rosel machen / Also nement
eyn lot presilie geschaben oder gestossen und
uud die menisteren krense In die presilie gabe
an der mittel der krense gange und nement dan
lut starck lauge und werme sy Do sol lebe
sy und gysset sie uber die presilie die lange
eyn quinte uniger uber die presilie gange und
ruret es dan wol und lemender von menisch

dan uff stunde eyn quinzin schriben kride und ruret
die dar zu und uff stunde so habet eyn halb lot und
gebranten alun und der ... auch dar under
und nemet dan war ob es sich zu snut uff hebe
also es schumen wolt und lont es stan drey oder
vier oder funff tage so ir es lenger stan lont so
es bruner wirt und gisset es dan in eyn herte
kride durch eyn duch und lont es trucken Dar
nach so riben es mit lutern gumy gumy nit zu
starck und auch nit zu kranck zu glicher wyse also
blo an daude

nö bestet rosel
Das licht rosel sullet ir machen also nement das
preselien kole der ir ns gesiben hant und in dem
buch glieben ist das duit widder in die krense und
giessent ob es lauten die mit zu heiss sy dar uber
als vor und nemet dan uff vier oder funff lo ge-
ribner kride und duit die dar under und
weiss alun // diss ruten wol under nander und
lont es stan eyn nacht oder zwo und gisset es
dar uff also das satte rosel und ribe es dan so
so es wol trucken worden ist zu glich wyse also
hatt rosel

nö bly ... blugel
Das bly wiss und das bly gel die bede sullet
ir in mol wol riben mit lutern gumy arabisch
wasser und sullet es auch da mit temperen
das es nit zu starck sy und auch nit zu kranck
und in der dicke das es uffer dem bensel gange
und sullet auch sy alle zit mit eim saffery
vinger under riben so ir su bruchen wollent

nö grin
Berg grin oder schiffer grin das sullet ir uber
nacht beyssen in gebranten win oder in essig oder
sust in guten starcken wissen win das der win

den grünen eslich erauet mit der vber vnd riben
es dan vff ein bleie stein recht wol vnd dunt
dar vnder ein wenig bli gel ye me ir bli gel dar
vnder dunt so es we gel sar oder lauff für
vnde vnd wollet ir hast grün haben so
dunt ein weiß saff grün dar vnder oder
nement das paff von roten kride auch so
moget ir der vnder riben ein wenig wiß
win stein So behaltes By es der krauen vnd
wol es wol gerriben ist So temperan es dan
mit win oder mit essig vnd ein wenig ef en
wasser dar vnder nit zu starck vnd lant
es stan So es gantz trucken wirt vnd neues
es dan aber mit win vnd bruchst es

grün saft grün
Das saff grün sullet ir me riben wedder
uff ein stein noch uff ein glase noch
mit ein vmeser gießet luter wasser dar
übe ein wenig vnd daz saff lant setterlich
dar uff gan vnd dan es kunt in da dicke
als ein dinte do mit mu ez riche schribet
So ist daz saff gerecht n sullet es mit ein
bensel uff streichen | nü azynnige

nü azynnige
ye azynnige sullen ir wol riben mit dem
wyß oder mit grüm clauß vnd temperet
es dan mit lutern wasser also daz sie nit
zu kranck werde Dye azynnige wa nit auch
geen dicke nach dem riben lant sie er riu
ten vnd temperet sie dan es get n abe
vnd so dicker so besser vnd strichent sie
dan uff mit einem bensel ⊣ Swartz

nö
Das kern swartz ist daz beste uff illuaren
Sie sullen ir vierczehe dage dronken vnd
alle tage daz waß abe schütten vnd feisth
luter buen claß dar über vnd sullent es
dan erchte wol riben mit gum claß vnd
auch do mit temperie nit zu starck daz es
uffer die seiden gange es golt vmb zu strache

hime warbe
Dye hime warbe die mache also nement grit
mellbeth blo daz vast cleyn sy vnd dut dar
vnder satt roß oder roun ober vnd bli
dut tempiced zu same so ist es sein
wyß dut tempicees zu same so ist es sein
woller ir es liecht habe Das liet an dem
bli claß Wollet ir es satt han daz lit an
roß woller ir es blo wart han das lit an
dem blo vnd temperen es also daz roß
dem blo vnd temperen mit gum claß ⊣ Wye ma alle varbe
schettelbe sal vnd lbo mit // vnd vorhohen

sal vnd auch lbo mit

nö
Das blo Das azure musird daz roß daz so
liecht ist grun azynge vnd hime dise
varbe alle sal ma schettelbe vnd auch
vohohen zu glicher wyse also do vorna
stat von dem lop werck geschreiben
vnd auch gemolt

nö
bly wyß vnd bli gel mögen ir abe schette
We mit satten roß oder mit saff grün
oder mit ein dunen swarge vnd daz
bli wyß schohen mit bli gel Dyß snt
die dote varbe dar uff ma schetteuber
vnd auch vorhohent Rof

[6v]

Blo daz vast liecht ist az ynthe die liecht ist
vol daz liecht ist berg grün schiffer grün
zuze andern mischen bly, daz bly geit dise
varben alle sullen wir anstreichen uff daz
dünst daz wir künd daz es doch ein grüns
varbe sy uff gestrichen. Auch sullent ir
alle varbe ein mal wol riben die zu ribe
sint also do vor nun statt. Auch sullent ir
merken daz die varben wol temperiert sint
mit gumy wasz nit zu starck und mit zubrung
Auch sullen wir alle varbe uff tragen anstreiche
schenen und uhohen mit dem bensel an ir
feldung die sullen wir an streiche mit der
federn und uhohen mit den besl. Tust
alles löpwerck odn blumwerck mit
eym bensel gross und clein
Auch sullent ir uff kein varbe schettelbe odn
verhohen die underrarg sy daz zu mal
wol truken werden daz kein varbe in die
andern ganget. Auch sullet ir kein varben
anstreichen ir haben dan die varben vor
huen wol durch netzet und wol durch
nasz sy in der dicke also do vor geschriebe stet
az recht ein daz ir daz gumy wasz nit zu
starck mache sullet und sullet es auch alle
zyt suber und kein halte stoszs und mit
lieber es vier feldung dar uff gen daz
merteyl alle feldung zel
Wer sullet ir nun te so ir wollet ein feldung
mache in buchstaben odn m bildung so
sullet ir die feldung vor hien linierien
und ir glaichet so sie beh stat mit einer
dünen wasz recht durch dienet zu starck sy

[7r]

ye sullet auch daz bunet suffen mit ein virte
blosem ab fremst dar uff so bald odn teut
dan solich dinng daz hundert den zan an dem
gulde dar nach so wir es gesuffet hunt und
getempert so uber lauffet es mit eym zan
daz die har an dem bunet sich glich legent
auch so sullet ir den gold grün in die feldung
alleweg an streichen mit ein federn und mit
mit eyn bensel ir varbez, in die verdung auch
mit ein federn ir sullet oba die verdung uho
hen mit eym bensel. Auch so megent wir gar
vil feldung uff der feldung beenge mit under
inge die varben die scho ffzabel feldung
die sulo ir linyeren und mit golt grün an
streichen und reguleiren also ir i hiesz zwei
englen scher

Dar nach so nenet sait rosel daz es schon ist
und temperee es mit gumy wasz daz es uff
der federn gunge und streichet dan uber art
eyn linger an, vn uber zwo eyn uber art also
daz ir uber art zwo linge lee ston und dar
nach eyn linge gesullerin und aber zwo lee
und aber eyn gesullet biss ende uff also hie
in dem ersten nechste engel merklich stot
und zu glich wise dar nach in dem engel
dar uber so vinket ir also ir in dem nesten
vir art eyn lingr gesullet han mit rosel in
zwo lingr han lassen lee stan, vnd daz hunt

geton uff ein site zu glich wise so machet über
act gegen den lingen dar nach aber ein vnd
zwo lant lee stan also ye hie in er ander ringe
sind Daz er vier blibet wiß vnd lee stan
vnd nemet eben wan daz er mit feder en
strichen wan also er han gestrichen in dem
erst nach yen ringe gegen der rechten hant
also strichen er muß in dem andern ringe gegē
die lincken hant Also hie vnd mit er nach ye
han den ende ens ober zwei lee blibent
stan wan es gebürt sich also ꝛc.

¶ Dar nach so machet ab mit ein feder en blo vbant
ein lee ringe uff er vier an ein also in diesen
nach ringeln stot ym nechsten vnd lang aber
ein ringe über act lee stan vnd fullet dye
ander also hie mit blo vnd zu glich wise so
fullet Die oberge vier besset vier mit rott vnd
hie mit grün vnd aber vier mit grün bess
uff also in dem andern ringeln stott

¶ Dar nach so nemet blau es vnd lingeret mit ein
feder en die feld ding nach eme ist Daz krey swarz
sal dune sin dz es grün uff er die feder en gange

---

die feder sal warch sin es mit durch streichet die
feld er rein daz ma vnderscheid lichet die
golt vnd die varbe sehen möge vnd machet
daz mit dem swarzen in est blo daz rot vn
in daz grün ein creutzel also hie stot in den
nesten ringel vnd dar nach so nemet eine
bensel vnd nemet blau wiß machet spar acy
in die rosel varbe vnd ziehent sie zu same
also hie in dem andern ringel

¶ Dar nach so nemet aber blau wiß vnd machet
mit ein bensel in dz blau rosechen also in den
nechsten ringel stat vnd dar nach mit dem
gelen in die roten vnd grüne auch ros echen
also in den andern ringel stot ꝛc

¶ Dieß ist die ander feld ding die füllet er lingret
an strichen vn er füllet also hie in diesen obē
ringel statt Dar nach streichet es an mit
saur rosel also hie stot über act ne über ens
mit ein feder en vn ab über act mit rosel ge
ge lwarch also er dz in er andern ringel stot
hie nest vn füllet es fünff bliben stan

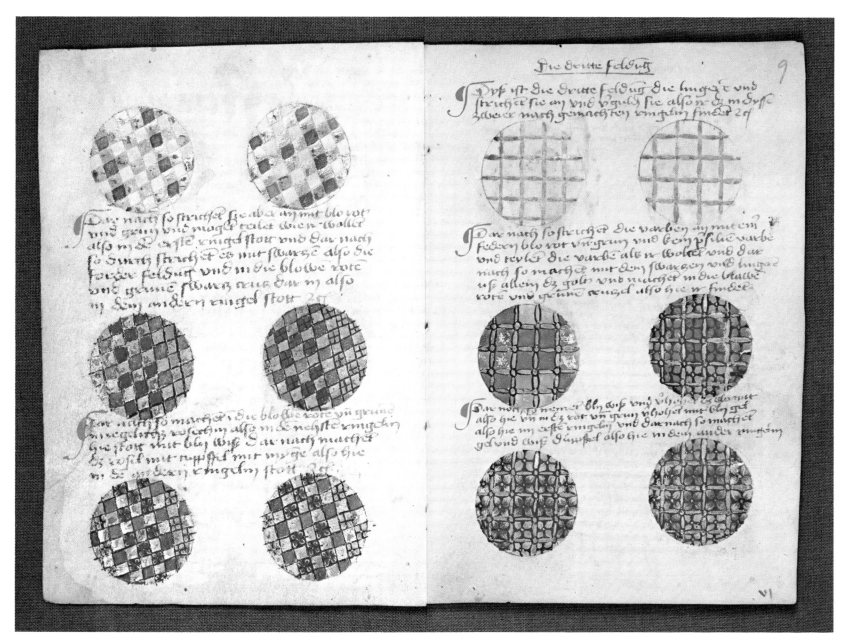

[8v]

[9r]

Diß ist die vierde feldung die linipod vnd vergulß also
ne die forder feldug gemacht hat vn streicht an
slecht blo vnd far roßel vnd durch streicht sie mit
swarcz vñ machet in dz blo weiß odr in var dupffel
vnd in dz roßel weiß odr rot dupffel also hie stot

nō aueu
musteu

Es nemet ein lot zin dz do wol ist geruket vnd dur
den in ein goltsmid tigel vn lant es wol zergan uff
kalen vn nemet dan ij lot quecksilber die auch
gelutert ist vn gisset den quecksilber in den zinlafen
zin ob dem fure vn rurt es das vndereinander wit
ein reor odr geissel vnd hand es dan von dem fure
vn lant es kalt werden vnd dar nach so ribet es
uff ein ribe stein rechte clein vnd flosset es dan
mit lutem wasser biß dz es schon do von gert dar
nach so nemet es vnd sprente es an dusine uff ein
bret oder uff ein bapier odr wo uff ir wollet
ist es wider kalt so lant es druken werden rechte
wol dar nach so nemet ij lot salarmoniatum vn
ij lot lebendig sclwebel glich vil die reben auch zu
same vn rut vnder den zin ij odr quecksilber also
hant ir acht lot zusamd vier lot by ein dar ist
zin vñ quecksilber in dem ab vier lot vn em dz
ist sal armoniatu vn lebendig sclwebel dar nach so
nemet ein woge vn wiget die ersten vier lot zin
vn quecksilber syt es dan glich vier lot zu samen
so nemet dan die ander vier lot sal armoniatu
vn lebendig sclwebel daz es auch vier lot werden diß
alles zu samen in quecksilber sal armoniatu vn
lebendig sclwebel dz ist viij lot zusamen dar nach so
nemet ein glas es do heisset ein muuel daz groß
sy daz glaß beslaget mit lutem leymē vn
rij oder mist vn salz wol geslage es slaget dar

---

umb daz glaß halb querck vn gar dicke biß
an den halß vnd lant es wol trucken dar nach
so nemet die acht lott vn gut sie in ein glaß
vn sal daz also groß sy dz die spes die acht lot
mr an daz mittel des glaß gange vn machet
ein holzel oben in dz glaß vnd nemet dan
ein haffen der so groß sy dz daz glaß sothet
dar in gange odur ne moget nemet ein groß
scherben vnd vmb kleubet die auch wol mit
dem vorgenante leyme vnd lant ij trucken
dar nach so nemet kleine sant odur gestube
esche vnd sezet daz glaß mit der spes in den
haffen odur scherben vnd den sant odur die
esche dar vmb biß an den halß vn sezt
dz uff ein treffuß odr uff ein stein vn machet
dar vnder vnd dar vmb ein fure mit kole
zum ersten gar senfft biß daz die spes zur
gehet vnd lant das glaß oben offen biß
das kein erruch dar uß gange vnd lant
es also boren in ein steten fure vij
stunden vnd lant es dan von ym selbes
kalt werden vnd betchent dan daz glaß
uff so hant ir es ob got wol gut auer mu
sind daz auruu musteru ribent vnd
temperieren also do vorna gescheehen
stott Rc

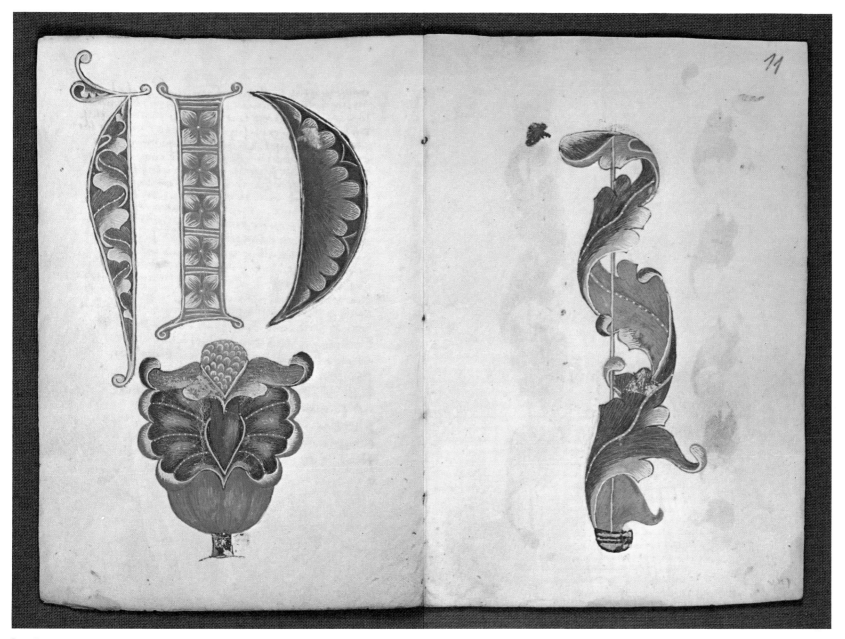

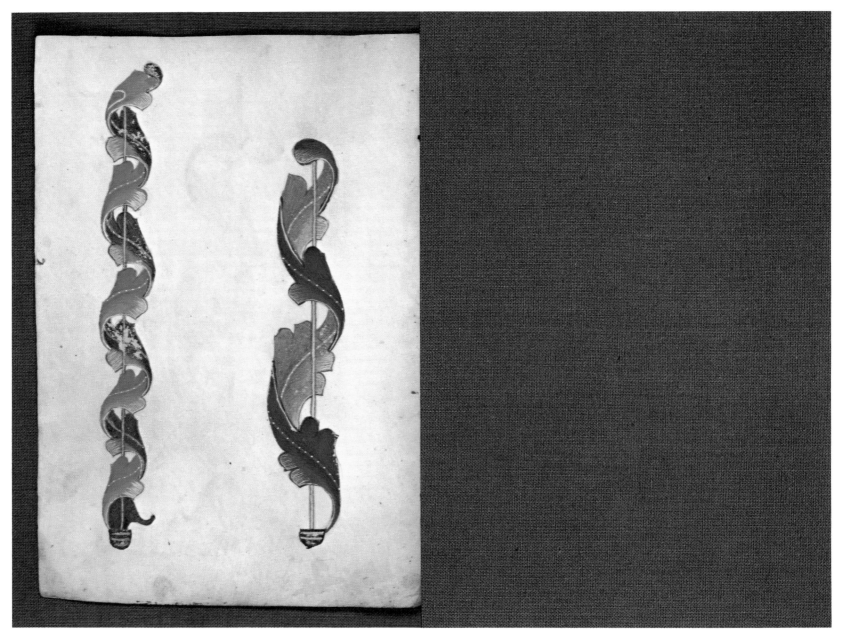

The main purpose of this translation is to provide an easily readable and understandable text of GMB for bibliophiles and bibliographers alike, for students of medieval book illumination, art historians, and other scholars. For the specialist who would like to examine the original text, the facsimile is in hand. The translation is as literal as possible and as free as necessary. No special attempt was made to preserve the archaic flavor of the original, but where clearly understandable, some archaisms were left standing. As far as possible I have tried to preserve the original order of words and of lines. This ordering will make it easy for the specialist to locate lines in the facsimile of the original.

Some obvious scribal errors were corrected, as well as what appear to be outright mistakes and duplications. A number of passages are most difficult to understand, and in one or two places the meaning remains indecipherable. I made reasonable efforts to cope with these difficulties to the extent of my abilities, always with the aim in mind of presenting a readable text. Certain passages, for instance in the description of the checkered or chessboard backgrounds, are best understood when read against the corresponding illustrations in the facsimile.

Some of the ambiguities and difficulties need explanation, usually in reference to the words of the original. My notes, I trust, will clarify these matters for the reader.

The original text bears very little interpunctuation. Occasionally one finds a period to indicate the end of a sentence and the beginning of the next; many sentences begin without any interpunctuation. In these cases the reader will find a semicolon, inserted in order to render the text more easily readable. This practice has been followed in the German and in the English translations. Emphases indicated by underlining in the original Model Book are rendered in italic in the modern versions.

[1r]   *Laub Werk*
      Das Laub soll man zuerst mit einem Blei oder
mit einem Stifft entwerffen. Danach soll man
das Laub umreiszen mit einer Feder und mit
sehr dünner Tinte oder mit dünner schwarzer Farbe.
Danach soll man das Laub glätten mit einem
Zahn, so dasz die Farbe glatt darauf liegen wird,
aber nicht zu fest. Danach soll man es anstreichen
mit den Farben, eine Seite rechts und die andere
Seite links oder verkehrt, mit einem Pinsel, nämlich
lichtrot und grün, das heiszt berggrün oder
schiefergrün: Die zwei Farben gehören zusammen, die eine Seite lichtrot und den Umschlag[1]
grün, wie hier gezeigt, oder die eine Seite grün den Umschlag lichtrot, wie Du willst.   §

      Danach so nehmet sattrote Farbe und um-
reiszet das Lichtrot mit dem satten Rot
mit einem Pinsel, gleichsam als ob Ihr
es noch einmal umreiszen wolltet, um
das Rot auswendig herum. Danach so
nehmet Saftgrün und umreiszet das Berggrün oder das Schiefergrün mit dem Saftgrün, in gleicher Weise wie mit dem Rot,
ringsherum. Danach so machet mit
einem Pinsel und mit dem satten Rot

1. *Umschlag* in the original: the reverse of the leaf.

[IV]

einen Grat mitten durch das Laub, das damit Lichtrot angestrichen ist, und mit
dem Saftgrün, auch mit einem Pinsel, einen
Grat mitten durch das Berg-oder Schiefergrün, wie es hier dargestellt ist. §

Danach so nehmet abermals das Sattrot und
mischet es dünner auf der Hand oder in einer
Muschel mit lauterem dünnen Gummi-Wasser,
dasz es dann wirklich dünner sei, wir hier gezeigt: § ☐ [2]
Danach so nehmet dasselbe dünne Sattrot
für eine Seite, nämlich den Umwurff des Blattes,
oder für die Rückseite, wie es hier dargestellt ist. Danach so nehmet Saftgrün und mischet
es dünner mit lauterem Brunnenwasser auf der
Hand, oder worin Ihr wollt, dasz es auch
wirklich dünner sei, wie es hier dargestellt ist. ☐ [2] Danach so streichet auf mit einem Pinsel
das Grün, wie es hier dargestellt ist.

2. These are two somewhat faded color samples; see the facsimile.

3. I have kept the original *temperieren* (Middle High German, according to Grimm) in the German translation. It denotes the mixing of colors to their proper consistency.

Danach nehmet abermals Sattrot und temperieret[3] es mit Gummi-Wasser, nicht zu stark

[2r] und auch nicht zu dünn, also eine Tinte, die nicht
zu dünn ist, so dasz sie leicht aus dem Pinsel fliesze. Damit
schattieret das Lichtrot, nämlich mit dem
wässrigen Rot, mit kleinen Strichen, wie es hier dargestellt ist.
Danach so nehmet Saftgrün und temperieret
es mit lauterem Wasser, aber rühret es nicht mit
dem Finger, sondern laszet die Flüssigkeit von selbst zergehen,
dasz sie so dick sei wie eine dünne Tinte.
Damit schattieret Ihr das Berggrün, nämlich mit
dem wässrigen Saftgrün in derselben Weise
wie das Rot, und wie es hier dargestellt ist.

Danach so nehmet Bleiweisz, das wohl gerieben sei, und höhet das Lichtrot mit einem
Pinsel auf den schattierten Teil des Blattes
oder des Laubes, und so, dasz die Strichlein
in Weisz kleiner sind,[4] wie hier dargestellt ist.
Danach so machet auf den Grat, der
da zweifaltig sein soll, mit dem
Pinsel und dem Bleiweisz kleine Tüpfe-
lein, wie es hier dargestellt ist.

4. At this point the original has *so sie basz
stat*, which I do not understand and therefore
cannot translate.

[2v]

Danach so machet in das Grün, auch in den
Grat, Tüpfel, und dafür nehmet wohlgeriebenes Bleigelb, temperiert mit Gummi, so dasz es gut aus
dem Pinsel fliesze. Das Bleigelb ist nicht für das
Rot bestimmt, sondern für das Grün.
Das ist besser auf Grün, das ist das Beste.
Danach so höhet das grüne Laub auf
der andern Seite gegen die grüne Schattierung zu
mit Bleigelb, in gleicher Weise wie das Rot
mit dem Bleiweisz, so hier das Grün mit dem
Bleigelb, wie es hier dargestellt ist.   §

Nota Mennig
und Purpur

Mennig und Purpur, diese zwei Farben
gehören zusammen auf dem Laubwerk, eins
rechts und die andere Seite links; und
Ihr sollet das Laub vorher entwerffen mit
einem Blei, danach nachreiszen mit einer Feder, und danach mit der Mennige-oder
der Purpurfarbe anstreichen, eine Seite Mennig
oder Purpur und den Umschlag Purpur oder
Mennig, wie Ihr wollt, wie es hier dargestellt ist.

[3r]

Danach so nehmet Rot und umstreichet die
Mennig-und die Purpurfarbe, beide ringsherum, mit einem Pinsel, und machet einen zwei-
fachen Grat mitten auf das Laub,
wie es hier dargestellt ist.

Danach nehmet abermals das Sattrot und
machet es gehörig dünner mit lauterem Gummi-
wasser, ebenso wie das licht-
rot, wie es oben beschrieben ist, und streichet die
beiden Farben damit an und schattieret sie, wie hier.

Danach so nehmet abermals Sattrot und schattieret damit,[5] wie es vorher dargestellt ist, das
Lichtrot, wie es hier dargestellt ist.

Danach so höhet das Purpur mit Bleiweisz und
verhöhet die Mennig mit Bleigelb, wie es hier dargestellt ist.

5. It is not clear from the text which of the
two reds mentioned is to be shaded and which is
to be used for the shading.

[3v]
Nota Blau
und Aurum
musicum

Blau und Aurum musicum, die zwei Farben gehören
zusammen an dem Laubwerk, eine rechts, die
andere links. Ihr sollt auch hier wieder das Laubwerk
zuerst entwerffen und dann umreiszen mit
einer Feder mit dünner schwarzer Farbe oder mit dünner
Tinte, dann polieren; und danach mit dem
Blau oder mit Aurum musicum anstreichen, eine Seite
blau, die Unterseite Aurum musicum, wie Ihr es
dann einteilen wollt, wie es hier dargestellt ist.

Danach so umreiszet sie beide mit Sattrot rings herum, nämlich die obengenannten zwei
Farben, und wie es hier dargestellt ist.

Danach nehmet abermals Sattrot und verdünnt es, und
schattieret die beiden Farben damit in derselben Weise
wie die Mennig und das Purpur, wie es hier dargestellt ist.

Danach schattieret sie basz ab mit dem Rot abenso
wie die vorhergenannten Farben, wie es hier dargestellt ist.

[4r] Danach so nehmet Bleiweisz, und mit einem kleinen
Pinsel höhet die beiden Farben damit,
wie es oben steht und wie es hier dargestellt ist.

Das assis oder der grosze Goldgrund, den
machet also: Holet geriebene Kreide, die
gut gerieben sei und auch gut trocken geworden
ist, bei einem Maler. Dieselbe Kreide, reibt sie
noch einmal auf einem Reibstein mit wohlgeschlagenem
Eiweisz; und holet dann Bolum armenum[6]
in der Apotheke, und reibet so viel darunter,
dasz die Kreide davon eine rote Fleischfarbe gewinne.
Ist nun von der Kreide so viel da wie eine kleine Bohnen
nusz,[7] so nehmet von dem Bolus so viel wie eine kleine
Haselnusz und reibet ihn wohl unter die Kreide mit
dem Eiweisz; und nehmet dann Zuckerkand,
so viel wie eine halbe Haselnusz, also halb so
viel wie von dem Bolus; und nehmet dann Zinnober so viel wie
eine halbe Erbse. Dasz alles reibet recht wohl zusammen mit Eiweisz, dasz es wie ein Schmalz werde,
und tut es dann in ein Horn, das sauber sei,[8] und rühret
es mit einem Hölzel untereinander und temperieret es
in der Dicke wie ein Zinnober, dasz es leicht aus der Feder
fliesze; und laszt es sich dann untereinander beizen
und tut immer wieder Eiweisz darein, bis dasz es
gut beizet, und rühret es wohl untereinander; und laszt es
drei oder vier Tage stehen, und je länger es steht,
desto besser ist und wird es.[9] §

6. *Bolum armenum*: explained by Dr. Will in a
note to his transcript as the finest quality of the
red bolus, a fine-grained fat clay, which had been
used since antiquity to fix gold on wood.

7. The original text has *bon nusz*, but this is
probably a scribal error for *baum nusz*, evidently
meaning walnut.

8. The original has *schon = schön*, here used
for clean or pure.

9. The description of the preparation of the
gold ground ends here without any reference to
the application of the actual leaf gold.

[4v]

Wie Du alle Farben temperieren
und reiben sollest §

Blau sollet Ihr nicht reiben, es sei denn gar grob. Ist es grob, so reibet es auf einem Reibestein, der recht glatt sei, oder auf einer Glasscheibe oder auf einer Marmorplatte. Alsdann nehmet das Blau und leget es in lautere Lauge, über Nacht oder eine Stunde oder zwei, und reibet es dann auf einem Stein ohne die Lauge mit Eidotter. Danach so spült es recht wohl mit Lauge oder mit weiszem Wein oder mit lauterem Wasser, und laszt es dann auf einem Papier trocknen oder sonst in einem trockenen Geschirr. Wenn Ihr es lauter und schön und trocken ausgespült habt, dann nehmet lauteres Gummi-Arabicum-Wasser und temperieret es damit, dasz es leicht aus der Feder fliesze. Das Gummi-Wasser soll lauter sein, dasz es weder zu dick noch zu dünn sei und weder zu stark oder zu schwach sei, so dasz es richtig und auch nicht zu hell sei. Das Blau soll temperieret sein, dasz es leicht aus der Feder fliesze und aus dem Pinsel; und will es nicht herausflieszen, so nehmet ein wenig Zuckerkand, davon flieszet es leicht aus dem Pinsel.

Nota Aurum
musicum

Aurum musicum,[10] das sollet Ihr nicht fest reiben, Ihr sollet es reiben mit lauterem Brunnenwasser, und sollet es dann temperieren mit lauterem Gummi, so wie das Blau, ohne den Zucker. Ihr sollet es aber spülen mit lauterem Brunnenwasser und danach temperieren, wie es vorher geschrieben steht, nicht zu stark und auch nicht zu schwach. § / *Nota. Sattbraun oder Sattrot*

Das Sattbraun oder Sattrot machet also: Nehmet ein Lot Brasil-Holz,[11] geschabt oder gestoszen, und tut es in einen steinernen Krug, dasz das Brasilholz den Krug bis zur Mitte fülle; und nehmet dann lautere, starke Lauge und wärmet sie, dasz sie lau sei, und gieszet die Lauge über das Brasilholz, ein Finger breit darüber, und rühret es dann gut untereinander; und nehmet

10. *Aurum musicum* is a sort of imitation gold leaf, although it looks quite different here—a brownish tint with a light metallic sparkle. The term *musicum* does not refer to music, but is a latinized form of medieval German terms *Musiergold*, *muosiren*, to adorn, to decorate. It may also be related to *aurum mosaicum* or *musivum* (mosaic gold), used in gilding wood or metal, depending on the etymologist's point of reference. It is mentioned and discussed in German manuals on painting and dyeing. See Ploss, *op. cit.*, pp. 92, 97, 164, 166, 206. See also Thompson, *op. cit.*, p. 37, notes 50 and 51; also his *Materials of Medieval Painting* (London, 1936), p. 181 ff.

11. *Presilie* in the original means brazilwood, a source of red or yellowish-brown color.

[5r]   dann sogleich ein Quäntchen geriebene Kreide und rühret
die dazu und schabet sogleich ein halbes Lot
gebrannten Alaun; den rühret auch darunter
und sehet dann zu, ob es sogleich aufgehe,
als ob es schäumen wolle; und laszet es stehen drei oder
vier oder fünf Tage. So Ihr es länger stehen laszet, so
wird es bräuner; und gieszet es dann auf harte
Kreide durch ein Tuch // und laszet es trocknen. // Danach so reibet es mit lauterem dünnen Gummi, nicht zu
stark und auch nicht zu schwach, in derselben Weise
wie das Blau, ohne Zuckerkand.

Nota
Lichtrosa   Das Lichtrosa sollet Ihr also machen: Nehmet das
Brasil-Holz, das Ihr ausgetrocknet habt und das in dem
Tuch geblieben ist. Das tut wieder in den Krug und
gieszet Lauge, die nicht zu heiss sei, darüber,
wie zuvor; und nehmet dann vier oder fünf Lot geriebene Kreide und tut sie darunter, aber
kein Alaun. Dies rühret wohl untereinander und
laszet es stehen eine Nacht oder zwei, und gieszet es
aus so wie das Sattrosa, und reibet es dann,
wenn es gut trocken geworden ist, in derselben Weise wie
das Sattrosa.

Nota
Bleiweisz
und Bleigelb   Das Bleiweisz und das Bleigelb, die beiden sollet
Ihr zumal wohl reiben mit lauterem Gummi Arabicum
Wasser, und sollet es auch damit temperieren,
dasz es nicht zu stark sei und auch nicht su schwach,
und in der Dicke so, dasz es aus dem Pinsel fliesze;
und sollet sie auch alle Zeit mit einem sauberen
Finger untereinanderrühren, so Ihr sie brauchen wollet.

Nota Grün   Berggrün oder Schiefergrün, das sollet Ihr über
Nacht in Branntwein beizen oder in Essig oder
sonst in gutem starken Weiszwein // dasz der Wein

12. *Rüten Krüde* in modern German is
Rautenkraut. The term is used at different times
and in different places for a variety of plants. It
is impossible to furnish a botanically correct
identification without an analysis of the pigment.

13. After the words *win stein* (tartar) this line
becomes unintelligible.

[5v]

in derselben Menge sei wie das Grün, nicht mehr; und reibet
es dann auf einem Reibestein recht wohl, und tut
darunter ein wenig Bleigelb. Je mehr Ihr Bleigelb darunter tut, desto mehr gelbe Farbe oder Laubfarbe
wird daraus; und wollet Ihr bastgrün haben, so
tut ein wenig Saftgrün darunter oder
nehmet den Saft von Rautenkraut.¹² Auch
möget Ihr darunter rühren ein wenig weissen
Weinstein¹³   und
wenn es wohl gerieben ist, so temperieret es dann
mit Wein oder mit Essig und ein wenig Gummi-
wasser darunter, nicht zu stark; und laszet
es stehen, dasz es ganz trocken wird, und netzet
es dann abermals mit Wein und benutzet es dann.

Nota
Saftgrün

   Das Saftgrün sollet Ihr nicht reiben, weder
auf einem Stein noch auf einer Glasscheibe, noch
mit einem Finger. Gieszet ein wenig lauteres Wasser darüber, und laszet das Saftgrün sachte
zergehen, und wenn es so dick wird
wie eine Tinte, mit der man leicht schreiben kann,
so ist das Saftgrün richtig. Ihr sollet es mit einem
Pinsel aufstreichen. | *Nota Mennige*
   Die Mennige sollet Ihr wohl reiben mit Eiweisz oder mit Gummiwasser, und temperieret
sie dann mit lauterem Wasser, so dasz sie nicht
zu schwach werde. Die Mennige wird auch
gern dick nach dem Reiben. Laszet sie trocknen und temperieret sie bis sie zergeht,
und je dicker je besser; und streichet sie
dann auf mit einem Pinsel. | *Schwarz*

[6r]

Das Kienschwarz ist das beste zum Illuminieren.
Das sollet Ihr vierzehn Tage lang tränken und
alle Tage das Wasser abschütten und frisch
lauteres Brunnenwasser darüber schütten; und sollet es
dann recht wohl mit Gummiwasser reiben und
auch damit temperieren, nicht zu stark, dasz es leicht
aus der Feder fliesze, das Gold zu umstreichen.

Nota
Purpurfarbe

Die Purpurfarbe, die machet also: Nehmet gutes
mehliges Blau, das recht fein sei, und tut darunter Sattrosa oder Tournesol und Bleiweisz. Dies temperiert zusammen, so wird daraus Purpur.
Wollet Ihr es hell haben, nehmet mehr
Bleiweisz. Wollet Ihr es satt haben, nehmet mehr
Rosa. Wollet Ihr es blauer haben, so nehmet mehr von
dem Blau; und temperieret es dann wie das Rosa
mit Gummiwasser. // Wie man alle Farben
schattieren soll und womit // und höhen
soll und auch womit.

Nota

Das Blau, das Aurum musicum, das Rosa, das da
hell ist, Grün, Mennige und Purpur, diese
Farben alle soll man schattieren und auch
höhen in derselben Weise wie es vorher
von dem Laubwerk geschrieben steht
und auch gemalt ist.

Nota

Bleiweisz und Bleigelb möget Ihr abschattieren
mit Sattrosa oder mit Saftgrün[14]
oder mit einem dünnen Schwarz, und das
Bleiweisz mit Bleigelb höhen. Das sind
die toten Farben,[15] darauf man schattieret
und auch verhöhet.   §

14. The original, curiously enough, says to
shade the lead white and lead yellow with dark
red or with dark green.

15. *Die doten Farben*: In a note to his transcript
Dr. Will explains that lead white and lead yellow
are the colors used to represent the pallor of
death.

[6v]

Blau, das sehr hell ist, Mennige, die hell ist,
Rosa, das hell ist, Berggrün, Schiefergrün,
Purpur, Aurum musicum, Bleiweisz, Bleigelb, diese
Farben alle sollet Ihr so dünn
auftragen wie Ihr könnt, dasz es doch ein gleichmässiger
Farbauftrag sei. / Auch sollet Ihr
alle Farben zumal gut reiben, die zu reiben sind,
wie es vorher steht. / Auch sollet Ihr
darauf sehen, dasz die Farben wohl temperiert sind
mit Gummiwasser, nicht zu stark und nicht zu schwach.
/ Auch sollet Ihr alle Farben mit dem Pinsel auftragen, anstreichen,
schattieren und höhen, auszer in
den Feldungen, die sollet Ihr mit der Feder
anstreichen und mit dem Pinsel höhen. Sonst
alles Laubwerk oder Blumenwerk[16] mit
einem Pinsel grosz und klein.
/ Auch sollet Ihr keine Farbe schattieren oder
höhen, der vorige Farbauftrag sei denn schon
gut getrocknet, so dasz keine Farbe in die
andere überläuft. / Auch sollet Ihr keine Farben
auftragen, wenn Ihr nicht die Farben vor-
her wohl durchnässet habt, so dasz sie durch und durch
nasz seien in der Dicke, wie vorher geschrieben steht.
Merket, dasz Ihr das Gummiwasser nicht zu
stark machen sollet, auch sollet Ihr es alle
Zeit sauber und rein halten von Staub und es nicht
zudecken. Vier Feldungen, von denen die
Mehrzahl aller Feldungen ausgehen.[17] §

Nota Hier sollet Ihr aufmerken, so Ihr eine Feldung machen
wollet in Buchstaben oder in Bildern,[18] so
sollet Ihr die Feldung vorher linieren,
und je gleichmässiger[19] umso richtiger wird es, mit einer
dünnen wässerigen Tinte, die nicht zu stark sei.

16. It is possible that the mention of *blume(n) werk* refers to a lost portion of GMB.

17. This phrase, although not underlined, is the heading to the next section, which deals with the four checkered backgrounds.

18. This statement applies to backgrounds for initial letters and miniatures. The mention of pictures may also be a reference to a lost portion of GMB.

19. The original reads somewhat cryptically *und je glicher so sie basz stat.*

[7r] Ihr sollet auch das Pergament säubern mit einem Roggen-
brosam; darauf sei Kalk oder Kreide, aber kein Firnis,
denn solches Ding hindert den Zahn beim
Vergolden. Danach, wenn Ihr es gesäubert habet und
liniert, so glättet es mit einem Zahn,
dasz die Haare an dem Pergament sich gleichmäszig legen.
Auch sollet Ihr den Goldgrund in die Feldung
allewege mit einer Feder anstreichen und nicht
mit einem Pinsel und Farben in die Feldung auch
mit einer Feder. Ihr sollt aber die Feldung mit
einem Pinsel höhen. Auf diese Weise möget Ihr gar
viele Feldungen aus der Feldung mit anderer
Verteilung der Farben herausbringen. Die Schachbrettfeldung,
die sollet Ihr linieren und mit Goldgrund anstreichen und vergolden, wie Ihr es in diesen zwei
Kreisen sehet.

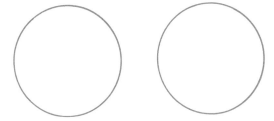

Danach so nehmet Sattrosa, das da rein ist,
und temperieret es mit Gummiwasser, dasz es leicht aus
der Feder fliesze; und streichet dann schräg[20]
eine Reihe an, und nach zwei Reihen wieder eine schräg, so
dasz je zwei schräge Reihen leerstehen, und danach
eine Reihe gefüllet sei und wieder zwei leer,
und wieder eine gefüllet, bis zum Schlusz, wie hier
in dem ersten nächsten Kreise deutlich dargestellt ist;[21]
und in gleicher Weise danach in dem Kreise
daneben, so findet Ihr dort
schräg eine Reihe gefüllet mit Rosa, und
zwei Reihen sind leergelaszen; und habet Ihr

20. The original uses the term *uber art* to mean, obviously, *diagonally.*

21. This description refers to the upper left circle on f.7v.

[7v] das getan auf einer Seite in gleicher Weise, so füllet schräg
gegen die Reihe danach wieder eines, und
zwei laszet leer stehen, wie Ihr es hier in dem nächsten Kreise
findet, dasz je vier weisz bleiben und leerstehen;
und nehmet Euch in acht, dasz Ihr nicht versäumet, anzu-
streichen. Wenn Ihr also in dem
ersten nahen Kreise nach rechts gestrichen habt,
so streichet Ihr nun in dem nächsten Kreise nach
links, wie es hier dargestellt ist, und beachtet,
dasz am Ende ein oder zwei leer stehenbleiben,
denn es gehört sich so.   §

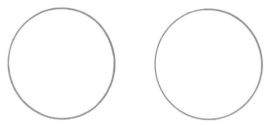

Danach so machet wieder mit einer Feder Blau schräg
in die leeren Reihen mit Ausnahme von je vieren, wie es in diesem
nächstfolgenden Kreise steht; und laszet wieder
eine schräge Reihe leerstehen und füllet dann die
nächste, wie hier dargestellt ist, mit Blau und gleichzeitig
füllet die übrigen Vierpässe mit Rot und
vier mit Grün, und wieder vier mit Grün, bis
zu Ende, wie es in dem anderen Kreise dargestellt ist.

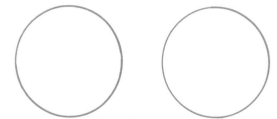

Danach so nehmet Schwarz und linieret mit einer
Feder die Feldung noch einmal. Das Kienschwarz
soll dünn sein, dasz es gern aus der Feder gehe.

[8r] Die Feder soll weich sein. Damit streichet säuberlich durch die
Feldung, dasz man unterschiedlich das
Gold und die Farbe sehen möge; und machet
dann mit dem Schwarzen in das Blau, das Rot und
in das Grün ein Kreuzel, wie es hier in dem
nächsten Kreise gezeigt ist; und danach so nehmet einen
Pinsel und nehmet Bleiweisz, machet Sparren
in die rosa Farbe, und ziehet sie zusammen,
wie hier in dem zweiten Kreise.

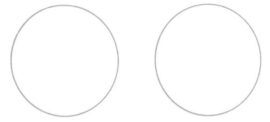

Danach so nehmet abermals Bleiweisz und machet
mit einem Pinsel in das Blau Röschen, wie es in dem
nächsten Kreise steht, und danach mit dem
Gelb in die roten und grünen Felder auch Röschen,
wie es in dem zweiten Kreise dargestellt ist.

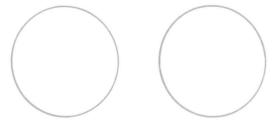

Dies ist die zweite Feldung. Die sollet Ihr linieren,
anstreichen und vergolden, wie es hier in diesen zwei
Kreisen steht.[22] Danach streichet sie an mit
Sattrosa, wie es hier steht, schräg jede zweite Reihe[23]
mit einer Feder, und wiederum schräg mit Rosa jede
andere Reihe, wie das in dem zweiten Kreise
hiernach steht; und es sollen je fünf stehenbleiben.

22. These instructions refer to the first two
circles on f.8v.

23. An examination of the two circles (f.8v)
will show more clearly what is meant here.
First, the rows are to be painted red diagonally
from the upper left to the lower right (first
circle) and then, from the lower left to the upper
right (second circle).

[8v]

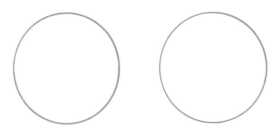

Danach streichet sie abermals an mit Blau, Rot
und Grün, und teilet es auf wie Ihr wollet,
wie es in dem ersten Kreise steht; und danach
so durchstreichet es mit Schwarz wie die
erste Feldung, und in die blauen, roten und
grünen Felder schwarze Kreuze hinein, wie es
in dem zweiten Kreise dargestellt ist.   §

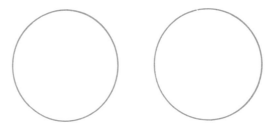

Danach so machet in alle die blauen, roten und grünen Felder
Röschen, wie es in dem nächsten Kreislein
hier steht, mit Bleiweisz. Danach machet
in das Rot Tüpfel mit Mennige,[24] wie es hier
in dem zweiten Kreislein steht.   §

24. In the fifth circle on f.8v the heightening of
the rosettes with lead white has disappeared
completely, and in the sixth circle the dots
applied with minium can be discerned only with
difficulty.

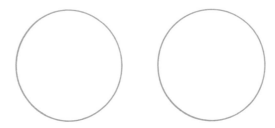

[9r]   *Die dritte Feldung*

Dies ist die dritte Feldung; die linieret und
streichet sie an und vergoldet sie, wie Ihr das in diesen
zwei hier folgenden Kreisen seht.   §

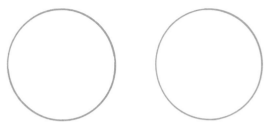

Danach so malt die Farben hinein mit einer
Feder, blau, rot und grün, aber keine Brasilholzfarbe,
und verteilt die Farben wie Ihr wollt; und danach nehmt das Schwarz und umreiszt
nur das Gold, und macht in die blauen,
roten und grünen [Felder] Kreuzchen, wie es hier steht.

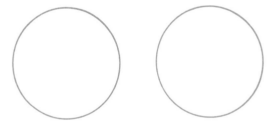

Danach so nehmet Bleiweisz und höhet das Blau damit,
wie hier [gezeigt]; und das Rot und Grün höhet mit Bleigelb,
wie hier im ersten Kreis gezeigt; und danach so machet
gelbe und weisze Tüpfel, wie hier im zweiten Kreis.

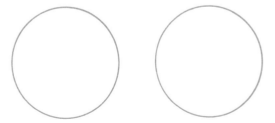

[9v]

Die vierte Feldung

    Dies ist die vierte Feldung; die linieret und vergoldet wie
Ihr die vorige Feldung gemacht habt, und streichet sie an
mit einfachem Blau und Sattrot, und durchstreichet sie mit
Schwarz; und machet in das Blau weisze oder rote Tüpfel,
und in das Rot weisze oder rote Tüpfel, wie hier steht.

Nota Aurum
musicum

    Nehmet II Lot Zinn, das da wohl gereinigt ist, und tut
das in einen Goldschmied-Tiegel und laszet es gut zergehen
über Kohlen; und nehmet dann II Lot Quecksilber, das auch
gereinigt ist, und gieszet das Quecksilber in das zerlaszene
Zinn über dem Feuer und rühret es dann untereinander mit
einem Draht oder Griffel, und nehmet es dann von dem Feuer
und laszet es kalt werden, und danach so reibet es
auf einem Reibestein recht klein und waschet es dann
mit reinem Wasser, bis dasz es gut flüssig ist. Danach so nehmet es und breitet es aus an der Sonne auf einem
Brett oder auf einem Papier oder worauf Ihr wollet.
Ist es nicht kalt, so laszet es recht gut trocken werden.
Danach so nehmet II Lot Salmiac und
II Lot lebendigen Schwefel,[25] dieselbe Menge. Die reibet auch zusammen, aber nicht unter das Zinn oder Quecksilber. Also
habet Ihr acht Lot zusammen, vier Lot zusammen das
Zinn und Quecksilber, und dann nochmals vier Lot zusammen,
nämlich Salmiac und lebenden Schwefel. Danach
so nehmet eine Waage und wiegt die ersten vier Lot Zinn
und Quecksilber. Sind es dann richtig vier Lot zusammen,
so nehmet dann die anderen vier Lot Salmiac
und lebenden Schwefel, dasz es auch vier Lot werden.
Alles zusammen, Zinn, Quecksilber, Salmiac, und
lebender Schwefel, das sind VIII Lot zusammen. Danach so
nehmet ein Glas, das da heiszet Kleine Nonne,[26] das grosz
sei. Das Glas beschlaget mit reinem Leim, mit
Pferdemist und mit wohlgeschlagenem Salz; das schlaget

25. "Live" sulphur means natural sulphur, as
it is found in the ground, rather than processed
sulphur.

26. The original has *nuñel*, which, according to
Dr. Will, means *Nonnlein*, or *little nun*.

[10r] um das Glas einen halben Finger dick bis
an den Hals und laszet es gut trocknen. Danach
so nehmet die acht Lot und tut sie in das Glas;
und soll dies so grosz sein, dasz die Mischung, die acht Lot,
nicht bis zur Mitte des Glases gehe; und machet
ein Hölzchen[27] oben in das Glas und nehmet dann
einen Hafen, der so grosz sei, dasz das Glas völlig
darein geht; oder Ihr möget nehmen einen groszen
Topf, und umklebet den auch wohl mit
dem vorhergenannten Leim und laszet ihn trocknen.
Danach so nehmet feinen Sand oder gesiebte
Asche und setzet das Glas mit der Mischung in den
Hafen oder Topf und den Sand oder die
Asche darum bis an den Hals; und setzet
dies auf einen Dreifusz oder auf einen Stein und machet
darunter und darum ein Feuer mit Kohle,
zuerst gar sanft, bis dasz die Mischung zer-
gehet; und laszet das Glas oben offen bis
dasz kein Rauch mehr daraus gehet, und laszet
es so brennen in einem steten Feuer XII
Stunden, und laszet es dann von selbst
kalt werden und brechet dann das Glas
auf, so habet Ihr will's Gott gutes Aurum musicum. Das Aurum musicum reibet und
temperieret wie es vorher geschrieben
stehet. §

27. The purpose and use of the *holczel*, *Hölzchen* (little piece of wood) is not explained in the text.

[10V]

[11r]

[11v]

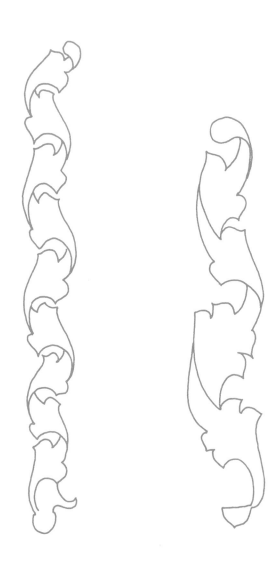

This English translation was made from the modern German version. It, too, aims to present a readable and easily understood rendering of the text of the Göttingen Model Book. My efforts to translate the German line for line raised some difficulties, since, in German, the verb frequently appears in a sentence in a position different from its place in English. As a result, more words deviate in this translation from their position in the original than in the German translation. Necessarily, this German translation and/or the original in the facsimile must be consulted by the specialist interested in the original text.

It has already been mentioned that ambiguities, errors, and difficult passages are commented upon in an apparatus of notes keyed to the text.

[1r]   *Foliage*

The foliage one shall first draw with a lead
or a point. Then one shall
outline the foliage with a pen and with
very thin ink or with thin black color.
Then one shall polish the foliage with a
tooth, so that the color can be applied smoothly,
but not too firmly. Then one shall paint it
with the colors, one side right and the
other side left or reversed, with a brush, namely
light red and green, that is to say green or
slate green: The two colors belong together, one side light red and the turnover[1]
green, as shown here, or one side green and the turnover light red, as you like.   §

Then take dark red color and outline the light red with the dark red
with a brush, so as if you
wanted to outline it once again, all around
the outside of the red. Then
take dark green and outline the green
or the slate green with the dark
green, the same way as with the red,
all around. Then make with
a brush and with the dark red

1. *Umschlag* in the original: the reverse of the leaf.

[IV]

the middle vein right through the foliage, which
is painted light red, and with
the dark green, also with a brush, the
middle vein right through the green or slate
green, as it is shown here. §

Then take again the dark red and
mix it thinner in the hand or in a
shell with pure, thin gum water,
so that it is really thinner, as shown here: § ▢ [2]
Then take the same thin dark red
for one side, namely the turnover of the leaf,
or of the reverse, as it is shown here. Then
take dark green and mix
it thinner with pure spring water in the
hand, or in whatever you wish, so that then
it is really thinner, as it is shown here: ▢ [2] Then
paint in the green with a brush,
as it is shown here.

Then take again dark red and temper[3] it with gum water, not too strong

2. These are two somewhat faded color
samples; see the facsimile.

3. I have kept the original *temperieren* (Middle
High German, according to Grimm) in the
German translation. It denotes the mixing of
colors to their proper consistency.

[2r] and also not too thin, that is to say an ink, which is not
too thin, so that it flows easily from the brush. With this
you shade the light red, namely with the
watery red, with little strokes, as it is shown here.
Then take dark green and temper
it with pure water, but do not stir it with
the finger, but let the fluid dissolve by itself,
that it gets as thick as thin ink.
With it you shade the green, namely with
the watery dark green, the same way
as the red, and as it is shown here.

Then take lead white, which shall be well
ground, and with it heighten the light red with a
brush on the shaded part of the leaf
or the foliage, and so, that the little strokes
of white are smaller,[4] as is shown here.
Then make on the middle vein, which
shall be a double line, with a
brush and the lead white little dots,
as it is shown here.

4. At this point the original has *so sie basz stat*,
which I do not understand and therefore cannot
translate.

[2v]

Then make dots into the green, also into the
middle vein, and for that take well-ground lead
yellow, temper it with gum, so that it flows easily
from the brush. The lead yellow is not meant for the
red, but for the green.
It is better on green, it is the best.
Then heighten the green foliage on the
other side towards the green shading
with lead yellow, in the same way as the red
with the lead white, so here the green with the
lead yellow, as it is shown here.   §

*Nota minium
and purple*

Minium and purple, these two colors
belong together on the foliage, one
on the right and the other side left; and
you shall first draw the foliage with
a lead, then retrace it with a pen,
and then paint in the minium or
the purple color, one side minium or
purple and the underside purple or
minium, as you like, as it is shown here.

[3r] Then take red and outline the
minium and the purple color, both all
around, with a brush, and draw a double
vein into the middle of the foliage,
as it is shown here.

Then take again the dark red and
thin it properly with pure gum
water, just as the light
red, as described above, and paint
both the colors with it and shade them, as shown here.

Then take again the dark red and shade
the light red with it,[5] as it is
described above, as shown here.

5. It is not clear from the text which of the
two reds mentioned is to be shaded and which is
to be used for the shading.

Then heighten the purple with lead white and
heighten the minium with lead yellow, as is shown here.

[3v]
Nota blue and aurum musicum

Blue and aurum musicum, the two colors belong together on the foliage, one on the right, the other on the left. Here, too, you shall first draw the foliage and then trace it with a pen with thin black color or with thin ink, then polish; and then paint with the blue or with aurum musicum, one side blue, the underside aurum musicum, as you want to arrange it, as it is shown here.

Then draw around both of them with dark red, all around, namely the above named two colors, as it is shown here.

Then take again dark red and thin it, and shade with it the two colors in the same way as the minium and the purple, as is shown here.

Then shade them with the red the same as the above named colors, as it is shown here.

[4r] After that take lead white, and with a small
brush you heighten both colors,
as it is written above and as it is shown here.

The assis or the great gold ground
you make thus: Fetch ground chalk, which
is ground well and is also well dried,
from a painter. This chalk, grind it
once more on a grindstone with well-beaten
egg white; and then fetch bolum armenum[6]
at the apothecary's, and grind so much into it,
that the chalk will turn a red flesh color therefrom.
If there is as much of the chalk there as a small tree
nut,[7] then take of the bolus, as much as a small
hazelnut and grind it well into the chalk with
the egg white; and then take sugar-candy
as much as half a hazelnut, that is to say half as
much as of the bolus; and then take cinnabar as much as
half a pea. Rub all this well to-
gether with the egg white, that it becomes like lard,
and then put it into a horn, which should be clean,[8] and stir
it with a small piece of wood and temper it
to the thickness of cinnabar, so that it flows easily
from the pen; and let it then macerate
and add again and again egg white, until it is
well macerated, and stir it well; and let it
stand three or four days, and the longer it stands,
the better it is and will be.[9] §

6. *Bolum armenum*: explained by Dr. Will in
a note to his transcript as the finest quality of
the red bolus, a fine-grained fat clay, which had
been used since antiquity to fix gold on wood.

7. The original text has *bon nusz*, but this is
probably a scribal error for *baum nusz*, evidently
meaning walnut.

8. The original has *schon = schön*, here used
for clean or pure.

9. The description of the preparation of the
gold ground ends here without any reference to
the application of the actual leaf gold.

[4v]

*How you shall temper all colors
and grind them §*

Blue you shall not grind, unless it is rather coarse.
If it is coarse, grind it on a grindstone, which should be
really smooth, or on a glass pane or a slab of
marble. Then take the blue and lay it into pure
lye, overnight or an hour or two, and
grind it then on a stone without the lye with egg
yolk. Then rinse it really well with lye
or with white wine or with pure water, and
let it then dry on a paper or in some
dry dish. When you have rinsed it clean
and fine and dried it, then take pure
gum arabic water and temper it therewith, that
it may flow easily from the pen. The gum water should be
pure, so that it is neither too thick nor too thin and neither
too strong nor too weak, so that it should be right
and also not too light. The blue should be tempered,
so that it flows easily from the pen and from the
brush; and if it does not want to flow, take
a little sugar-candy, that makes it flow easily from the brush.

*Nota aurum
musicum*

Aurum musicum,[10] you shall not grind it hard, you shall
grind it with pure well water, and then
you shall temper it with pure gum, like the blue,
without the sugar. But you shall rinse it with
pure well water and then temper it, as
it is written above, not too strong and also not
too weak. § / *Nota. Dark brown or dark red*

The dark brown or dark red make thus: Take
half an ounce of brazilwood,[11] grated or beaten, and
put it into a stone jar, that the brazilwood
fills half the jar; and then take
strong lye and warm it, that it is lukewarm,
and pour the lye over the brazilwood,
the width of a finger, and
stir it well; and take

10. *Aurum musicum* is a sort of imitation gold
leaf, although it looks quite different here—a
brownish tint with a light metallic sparkle. The
term *musicum* does not refer to music, but is a
latinized form of medieval German terms
Musiergold, muosiren, to adorn, to decorate. It
may also be related to *aurum mosaicum* or
musivum (mosaic gold), used in gilding wood or
metal, depending on the etymologist's point of
reference. It is mentioned and discussed in
German manuals on painting and dyeing. See
Ploss, *op. cit.,* pp. 92, 97, 164, 166, 206. See also
Thompson, *op. cit.,* p. 37, notes 50 and 51; also
his *Materials of Medieval Painting* (London, 1936),
p. 181 ff.

11. *Presilie* in the original means brazilwood,
a source of red or yellowish-brown color.

[5r] right away one-eighth ounce of ground chalk and stir
it in and grate right away a quarter ounce
of burnt alum; stir that in as well
and look and see whether it will dissolve right away,
as though it would foam; and let it stand three or
four or five days. If you let it stand longer, it
will get browner; and then pour it onto hard
chalk through a cloth // and let it dry. // Then
rub it with pure thin gum, not too
strong and also not too weak, in the same way
as the blue, without sugar-candy.

Nota light rose   The light rose you shall make thus: Take the
brazilwood, which you have dried out and which stayed
in the cloth. Put it back in the jar and
pour lye, which is not too hot, over it,
as before; and then take four or five ounces of
ground chalk and mix it in, but
no alum. Mix this well and
let it stand a night or two, and pour it
out like the dark red, and then grind it,
when it has dried well, in the same way as
the dark red.

Nota lead white and lead yellow   The lead white and the lead yellow, these two
you shall grind well with pure gum arabic
water, and you shall also temper it therewith,
that it be not too strong and also not too weak,
and of such thickness, that it flows from the brush;
and you shall always stir it with a clean
finger, when you want to use it.

Nota green   Mountain green or slate green, you shall
macerate it overnight in brandy or in vinegar or
else in a good strong white wine // that the wine

12. *Rüten Krüde* in modern German is *Rautenkraut*. The term is used at different times and in different places for a variety of plants. It is impossible to furnish a botanically correct identification without an analysis of the pigment.

13. After the words *win stein* (tartar) this line becomes unintelligible.

[5v]

be in the same amount as the green, not more; and then rub
it on a grindstone real well, and put
in a little lead yellow. The more you
add to it, the more yellow or leaf color
you will get; and if you want to get bast green,
add a little dark green to it or
take the juice of rue.[12] Also
you may stir in a little white
tartar[13]   and
when it is well ground, then temper it
with wine or vinegar and a little gum
water, not too strong; and let
it stand, that it gets quite dry, and wet
it again with wine and then use it.

Nota sap green

The sap green you shall not grind, not
on a stone nor on a glass pane, nor
with a finger. Pour a little pure water over
it, and let the sap green dissolve
gently, and when it gets as thick
as an ink, with which it is easy to write,
then the sap green is right. You shall put it on
with a brush. / *Nota red lead*

The red lead you shall grind well with egg
white or with gum water, and temper it
then with pure water but so that it
does not get too weak. The red lead tends to
get thick after grinding. Let it dry
and temper it until it dissolves,
and the thicker the better; and then put it on
with a brush. / *Black*

[6r]   The smoke black is the best for illuminating.
You shall soak it for fourteen days and
every day pour off the water and
pour pure well water over it; and you shall
grind it well with gum water and
temper it therewith, not too strong, that it
flows well from the pen, to outline the gold with it.

Nota purple   The purple color, make it thus: Take good
color   powdery blue, which is real fine, and add to
it dark rose or litmus and lead
white. Temper this together and it will turn purple.
If you want to have it light, take more
lead white. If you want to have it dark, take more of
the red. If you want to have it bluer, take more of
the blue; and then temper it like the rose
with gum water. // How one shall shade
all colors and with what // and shall heighten
them and with what.

Nota   The blue, the aurum musicum, the red, which
is light, green, minium and purple, all
these colors one shall shade and also
temper in the same way as it is described
previously for the foliage
and is depicted.

Nota   Lead white and lead yellow, shade with it
the dark rose or the dark green[14]
or use a thin black, and heighten
the lead white with the lead yellow. These are
the dead colors,[15] with which one shades
and heightens. §

14. The original, curiously enough, says to shade the lead white and lead yellow with dark red or with dark green.

15. *Die doten Farben*: In a note to his transcript Dr. Will explains that lead white and lead yellow are the colors used to represent the pallor of death.

[6v]

Blue, which is very light, lead red, which is light,
rose, which is light, mountain green, slate green,
purple, aurum musicum, lead white, lead yellow, all
these colors you shall apply as thinly
as you can, but still as an even
coat of color. | Also, you shall
grind well all colors, which are to be ground,
as it is written before. | Also, you shall
see to it, that the colors are well tempered
with gum water, not too strong and not too weak.
| Also, you shall apply all colors,
shade and heighten them, with the brush, except in
the checkered backgrounds, which you shall apply
with the pen and heighten with the brush. Otherwise,
all foliage or flower work[16] with
a brush large or small.
| Also you shall not shade or heighten
any color unless the previous coat of color is already
well dried, so that no color will
run into another one. | Also you shall not apply
any colors, unless you have first moistened
the colors well, so that they are wet through and through
in thickness, as is written before.
Watch that you don't make the gum water
too strong, and you shall keep it at all times
clean and pure from dust and not
cover it. Four checkered backgrounds, from which
the majority of all checkered backgrounds are derived.[17] §

Nota

Here you shall watch, when you want to make
a checkered background in letters or pictures,[18] you
shall first outline the checkered background,
and the more even[19] the better it will be
with a thin, watery ink, which is not too strong.

16. It is possible that the mention of *blume(n) werk* refers to a lost portion of GMB.

17. This phrase, although not underlined, is the heading to the next section, which deals with the four checkered backgrounds.

18. This statement applies to backgrounds for initial letters and miniatures. The mention of pictures may also be a reference to a lost portion of GMB.

19. The original reads somewhat cryptically *und je glicher so sie basz stat.*

[7r] Also, you shall clean the vellum with crumbs of
rye bread; over this should be lime or chalk, but no varnish,
for such a thing interrupts the tooth in
gilding. Then, when you have cleaned it and
outlined it, smooth it with a tooth,
so that the hairs on the vellum lie down smoothly.
Also you shall always put in the gold ground
into the checkered background with a pen and not
with a brush and the colors in the background also
with a pen. But you shall heighten the background with
a brush. In this way you may
develop many backgrounds out of the background
with a different distribution of the colors.
The chessboard background
you shall outline and draw in with gold ground
and gild it, as you see it in these two circles.

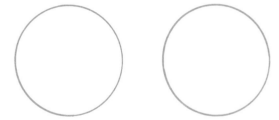

Then take dark rose, which is pure,
and temper it with gum water, so that it
flows readily from the pen; and then paint in one row
diagonally,[20] and after two rows one again diagonally, so
that two diagonal rows are always left empty, and after that
one row is filled and again two empty,
and again one filled, up to the end, as is clearly
shown here in the first of the following circles;[21]
and in the same way in the circle
next to it, you will find there
one diagonal row filled with rose, and
two rows are left open; and having done this

20. The original uses the term *uber art* to mean,
obviously, *diagonally*.

21. This description refers to the upper left
circle on f.7v.

[7v] on one side in the same way, then fill diagonally
against the row after that again one, and
let two stay empty, as you find it here in the next
circle, so that always four remain white and stay empty;
and take care, that you do not neglect to
fill in. When thus in the
first, nearest circle you have worked toward the right,
you must now in the next circle work toward
the left, as is shown here, and take care,
that at the end one or two stay empty,
for that is how it should be. §

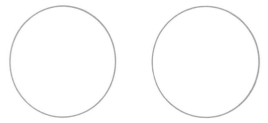

After that put again blue with a pen diagonally
into the empty rows excepting always four, as is shown
in the next following circle; and let again
one diagonal row stay empty and then fill the
next, as is shown here, with blue and at the same time
fill the remaining quatrefoils with red and
four with green, and again four with green, until
the end, as is shown in the other circle.

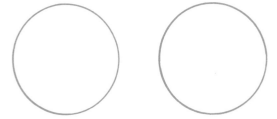

Then take black and outline the background
once more with a pen. The smoke black
shall be thin, so that it flows easily from the pen.

[8r] The pen should be soft. With it you must make neat strokes
through the background, that one can see
the gold and the colors separately; and then make
with the black a little cross into the blue, the red, and
the green, as it is shown here in the
next circle; and then take a
brush and take lead white, and make bars
into the rose color, and draw them together,
as here in the second circle.

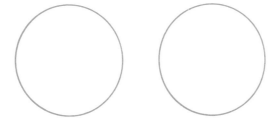

Then take once more lead white and make
rosettes with a brush into the blue, as it
is shown in the next circle, and then also with the
yellow rosettes into the red and green spaces,
as is shown in the second circle.

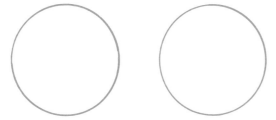

This is the second checkered background. You shall outline it,
paint and gild it, as it is shown here
in these two circles.[22] Then paint it with
dark rose, as is shown here, diagonally every second row[23]
with a pen, and again diagonally with rose every
other row, as is shown in the second circle
hereafter; and always five shall remain empty.

22. These instructions refer to the first two
circles on f.8v.

23. An examination of the two circles (f.8v)
will show more clearly what is meant here. First,
the rows are to be painted red diagonally from
the upper left to the lower right (first circle)
and then, from the lower left to the upper
right (second circle).

[8v]

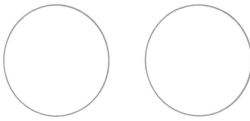

After that paint them again with blue, red,
and green, and divide the colors up as you like,
as is shown in the first circle; and after that
cross it through with black like in the
first checkered background, and into the blue, red, and
green spaces black color, as it
is shown in the second circle. §

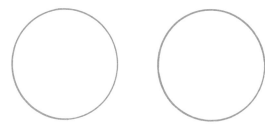

After that make rosettes into all the blue, red, and green
spaces, as it is shown here in the next little circle,
with lead white. After that make
into the red little dots with minium,[24] as it is
shown here in the second little circle. §

24. In the fifth circle on f.8v the heightening
of the rosettes with lead white has disappeared
completely, and in the sixth circle the dots
applied with minium can be discerned only with
difficulty.

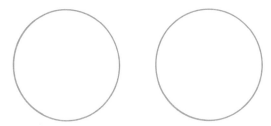

The Third Checkered Background

This is the third checkered background; outline it
and draw it and gild it, as you see it here
in the following two circles. §

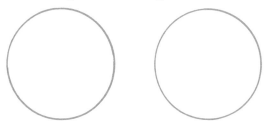

After that paint the colors in with a
pen, blue, red, and green, but no brazilwood color,
and distribute the colors as you please; and then
take the black and outline
only the gold, and put into the blue,
red, and green sections little crosses, as is shown here.

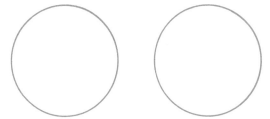

After that take lead white and heighten the blue with it,
as is shown here; and the red and green heighten with lead yellow,
as is shown here in the first circle; and after that make
yellow and white, as here in the second circle.

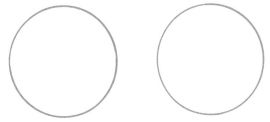

[9v]

The Fourth Checkered Background

This is the fourth checkered background; outline it and
gild it like you made the previous background, and paint it
with simple blue and dark red, and cross it through with
black; and make white and red dots into the blue,
and into the red, white or red dots, as is shown here.

Nota aurum musicum

Take one ounce of tin, which is well purified, and place
it into a goldsmith's melting pot and let it melt well
over coals; and then take one ounce of quicksilver, which is also
purified, and pour the quicksilver into the melted
tin over the fire and then stir it together with
a wire or stylus, and then take it off the fire
and let it grow cold, and after that grind it
on a grindstone very fine and then wash it
in pure water, until it flows readily. After
that, take it and spread it out in the sun on a
board or on a paper or whatever you like.
If it is not cold, let it dry real well.
After that take one ounce of sal ammoniac and
one ounce of live sulphur,[25] the same amount. These you also
grind together, but not with the tin and the quicksilver. Thus
you have together four ounces, two ounces
the tin and quicksilver together, and then once again two ounces
together, namely the sal ammoniac and the live sulphur. Then
take a scale and weigh the first two ounces of tin
and quicksilver. Then if it correctly makes two ounces,
take the other two ounces of sal ammoniac
and live sulphur, that it too makes two ounces.
Everything together, tin, quicksilver, sal ammoniac, and
live sulphur, that makes together four ounces. Then
take a glass which is called little nun,[26] which should be
large. The glass you cover with pure glue, with
horse manure, and with well-beaten salt; put that

25. "Live" sulphur means natural sulphur,
as it is found in the ground, rather than processed
sulphur.

26. The original has *nunel*, which, according
to Dr. Will, means *Nonnlein*, or *little nun*.

[10r] around the glass in the thickness of half a finger up
to the neck and let it dry well. Then
take the four ounces and put them into the glass;
and this should be so large, that the mixture, the four ounces
do not reach up to the middle of the glass; and put
a little piece of wood[27] into the top of the glass and take then
a pot, which should be so large, that the glass
fits into it completely; or you may take a large
pot, and it too you should cover well with
the above-mentioned glue and let it dry.
Then take fine sand or sifted
ashes and put the glass with the mixture into the
pot or the large pot and into the sand or the
ashes around it up to the neck; and place
this on a tripod or on a stone and make
under and around it a fire of coal,
gently at first, until the mixture melts;
and leave the glass open at the top until
no more smoke comes out of it, and let
it burn on a steady fire XII
hours, and let it then cool off
by itself and break open the glass,
and if God is willing you will have good aurum
musicum. The aurum musicum you grind and
temper it as is written
above. §

27. The purpose and use of the *holczel*, *Hölzchen* (little piece of wood) is not explained in the text.

[10V]

[11v]

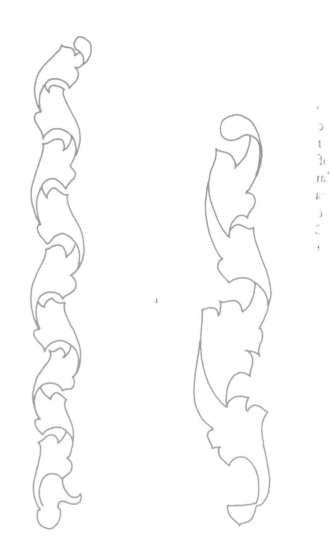

A number of manuscripts and printed books produced in Mainz in the middle of the fifteenth century show the influence of the Göttingen and Berlin model books. The quality of the illuminations taken from these model books is usually very high. The examples of borders and of checkered backgrounds and the suggestions for filling the strokes of larger initial letters are followed in most cases ingeniously and with a good deal of imagination without, however, disregarding the instructions of the two model books. It would be a very difficult undertaking to establish the identity of various hands. One would first need to assemble in one place all the volumes that followed the model books—which in itself would be practically impossible—in order to compare them and discover idiosyncrasies by which works could be attributed to certain artists. Further, the instructions in the model books are so explicit, so detailed, that quite possibly more than one hand may have executed illuminations without sufficient differentiation between them to fix the identification of several hands. For these reasons, this study does not greatly stress the identification of various hands. The reader may indeed find for himself some characteristic differentiations in the reproductions in this book.

As I suggested earlier, it is a unique situation that enables us not only to study a given model book but also to trace its direct influence in a sizable group of examples. I shall discuss these volumes in an order determined by geographic location, that is, in the order in which they might be examined by a hypothetical student who would start his journey in Göttingen or Berlin, then go south to Giessen, Frankfurt, and Mainz, and finally west to Paris and Washington.

The 42-line Bible in Göttingen is a very fine example of the use of the model books. It is one of the strangest coincidences in the history of books that both the Göttingen Model Book and this particular Gutenberg Bible should have become permanent holdings of the library in Göttingen. Both were, of course, together in Mainz over five hundred years ago—in 1454 or perhaps a year or two later, in the case of the Bible. After changes of ownership that we cannot trace in entirety, GMB was in the possession of Johann Friedrich A. von Uffenbach in Frankfurt until it came to Göttingen in 1769.

The Gutenberg Bible, printed and illuminated in Mainz, came to Göttingen via a totally different route. "This copy belonged originally to a monastery . . ., probably in the Kalenberg-Göttingen part of the Guelph domain; in the sixteenth century, in the possession of the estate of the Dukes, it was taken away from his realm after the death of Duke Erich (1584), by his illegitimate son Wilhelm but left behind in Fritzlar; after Wilhelm's death its return was demanded, and it was sent to Wolfenbüttel. . . . Together with the old Wolfenbüttel library, the Bible came to Helmstedt in 1614 and from there at the time of the Kingdom of Westphalia to Göttingen."[1] *Habent sua fata Libelli.*

The connection between GMB and the Gutenberg Bible was first noticed by the late Dr. Edmund Will[2] in the summer of 1939.

.   .   .   .   .

Let us now turn to a brief discussion of the volumes directly influenced by the model books. Since the Berlin Model Book has been unavailable for close study, I will be comparing these volumes specifically to the Göttingen Model Book.

GÖTTINGEN
Niedersächsische Staats- und Universitäts-Bibliothek

1. The 42-line Bible
2 volumes. Vellum. 2°.
Mainz, Johann Gutenberg, before 1454.
Seymour De Ricci, *Catalogue Raisonné des Premièrs Impressions de Mayence* (Mainz, 1911), No. 18; Edward Lazare, *The Gutenberg Bible: A Census* (Newark, N.J., 1956), No. 7; facsimile edition of B-42 (Leipzig, Insel-Verlag, 1913–1914), contains two illuminated pages of the Göttingen copy; Paul Schwenke, in the supplementary volume (*Ergänzungsband*) to the above-named facsimile edition, No. 5; facsimile edition from the Leipzig 1913–1914 facsimile (Pageant Press, Paterson, N.J., 1961); Don Cleveland Norman, *Pictorial Census of the Gutenberg Bible* (Chicago, Coverdale Press, 1961), No. 15. The reproduction of the illuminated pages, including the two from the Göttingen copy, are distinctly inferior to the Insel-Verlag facsimile.

Volume I contains c. 30, Volume II c. 80 initials and/or border decorations that follow the instructions and models of GMB very closely.

1. Translated from Paul Schwenke, *Ergänzungsband* (Leipzig, 1923).

2. Letter from Dr. Will to Professor Bruckner, Reinach near Basel.

The illuminator of this Gutenberg Bible made full use of GMB, of the various border decorations, the checkered backgrounds, the patterns for filling the stems of the larger initials and of the flower, as can be seen in figure 1. He did not always follow the colors of GMB but used other colors freely and with imagination. For instance, we find at times small portions of the leaf patterns inserted into the insides of initial letters. The illuminator observed a strict hierarchy in the position and size of the illuminations. As examples, the largest of the ornaments appear at the beginning of St. Jerome's introduction, at the beginning of the Old Testament, the Psalter, etc.; smaller initials and borders are used at the beginnings of the other introductions of St. Jerome (excepting the large initial mentioned above) and at the beginnings of the separate books of the Bible. In Volume II calligraphic pen work only is used on many initials. On f.5r of Volume I a piece of vellum that must have borne some fine illumination has been cut from the book.

GIESSEN

University Library

   2. The Butzbach Bible

Codex 653. 468 leaves. 2 columns, written in Frankish Bastarda. Paper. Large thick folio.

On the verso of the last, otherwise blank, leaf (also elsewhere in the codex): "Liber cap[itu]li Eccl[es]ie S[an]c[t]i Marci in Butzbach." Butzbach is a small town in Hessen, not far from Giessen. On the inside of the back cover two lines of writing, with itemized list of the production cost of the Bible (figures 11 and 12 and pages 91 and 92). "Completed in Mainz in November 1454."[3]

   The script is closely related to a Bible manuscript in the Municipal Archives in Mainz, Hs. II/61 (No. 7 in this list). The similarity is close enough to state with certainty that both manuscripts were written in the same scriptorium, and perhaps some portions by the same hand. A comparison of figures 11 and 12, illustrating this Bible, with figures 7, 8, and 13 (Mainz Old Testament) will reveal these similarities.

   Unfortunately, this codex has been so thoroughly cannibalized that it cannot be considered anything but a ruin. A handwritten notation dated 24.2.1967 reads: "List of the leaves damaged by cutting out of initials." (My translation.) All together, no less than 50 leaves are damaged or have been torn from the book. Further, the upper quarter of nearly all leaves shows damp stains, and the silver, which was used in many ornaments, has oxidized.

3. Schwenke, *op. cit.* My translation.

Although in principle I shall not stress the different hands as originators of the illuminations in a given volume, a word is in order for the Butzbach Bible. It is clear that not only are different hands distinguishable in the text, but also that the quality of the illuminations is generally somewhat lower than in GMB, with a few isolated exceptions.

However, there is no question that the directions and instructions of GMB were used for these remnants of the volume, with the high probability that they were followed, in general, for the stolen illuminations as well. It is clear that not every decoration is derived from GMB. Many of the plain initials were obviously executed without reference to GMB. The hierarchic principle observed in the Göttingen 42-line Bible is apparent also in the Butzbach Bible. The finely illuminated initials show clever use of GMB. Many are ornamented with checkered backgrounds exactly as described in GMB, while many others have the blossom or small segments of the leafy borders fitted into the background in the initial letters. One of the finest illuminated pages is on f.104r, where an initial *F* with very attractive checkered background, together with the typical leafy borders, graces the page.

FRANKFURT

Stadt- und Universitäts-Bibliothek
Four manuscripts with illumination closely related to GMB. These manuscripts were formerly in the Bartholomäus-Stift in Frankfurt (indicated as Barth.). They are described in detail by Georg Swarzenski and Rosy Schilling in their *Die illuminierten Handschriften und Einzelminiaturen des Mittelalters und der Renaissance in Frankfurter Besitz* (Frankfurt, Joseph Baer, 1929).

3. Missale Plenarium cum Calendario
Two columns. Latin, folio. Formerly property of Barth. (31). Swarzenski and Schilling No. 175.
Because of the evidence of the calendarium, the provenance, and the inclusion of coats of arms of Frankfurt families, Swarzenski and Schilling assigned this missal to a Frankfurt atelier, c. 1430–1466. There is actually no cogent reason why the manuscript could not have been illuminated in nearby Mainz. A client in Frankfurt could easily have commissioned the manuscript at a Mainz scriptorium and at the atelier of GMB for illuminations.

The missal, which is embellished with 17 initials and leafy borders, is a deluxe manuscript with beautifully colored decorations. One leaf at the beginning of the

Canon has been removed; it is almost certain that the leaf had on its verso the letter *T*, beginning the *Te igitur*. Here too, as in the Göttingen Gutenberg Bible, a hierarchy of size and decoration is observed, with very splendid decorations on, for examples, f.Ir, Xv, CXXVIr, CXLVIIIr, CLXXVIv, CCIXr. There is throughout a high quality of illumination. This missal belongs among the most exquisite examples of GMB influence, which is evident in figures 5 and 6.

4. Breviarium: Pars Hiemalis

Latin, folio. Formerly property of Barth. (40). Swarzenski and Schilling No. 176.
Assigned by Swarzenski and Schilling to the middle of the fifteenth century, originating in Frankfurt, and described as similar to No. 175, but rather more simple.
The tentative location in Frankfurt can be changed without any difficulty to Mainz. That the calendar fits Frankfurt use is no negative evidence for production in Mainz, nor is the fact that the manuscript was lent in the year 1482 by the Bartholomäus Library in Frankfurt a proof of Frankfurt origin.

Although the illumination is of high quality and generally dependent on GMB, some of the colors used do not appear in the Model Book, particularly a very dark blue, which was used in the initial letter in figure 2.

5. Breviarium: Pars Hiemalis et Aestivalis

Latin. 2 columns. 4°. Formerly property of Barth. (158). Swarzenski and Schilling No. 177.
Swarzenski and Schilling date the manuscript c. 1450–1460 and suggest its origin as Frankfurt. The criteria that support this attribution (Sunday letters and owner's notation) do not necessarily assign the manuscript to Frankfurt rather than Mainz.

In accordance with the 4° format, the decorations are usually smaller than in No. 175, though otherwise most of them are closely related. The reduction in size as well as the derivation from GMB is clear in figures 3 and 4. On some pages the initials are true to GMB, but the marginal decorations are quite different. The backgrounds of the initials on 6 leaves (between 36v–77v) are not filled with the circular examples of GMB, but with a blossom derived from the blossom on f.10v of GMB.

6. Petri de Braco Compendium Juris Canonici. (S. XIV)

Latin. 2 columns. Large folio. Praedicat. 59. Dominican Monastery. Swarzenski and Schilling No. 178.
The codex was written in Italy and the illumination added later in Mainz. Swarzenski and Schilling date this manuscript c. 1450–1460 and assign the illumination to Frankfurt, also noting the connection between this codex and their No. 175. The illumination here, too, is of very high quality.

MAINZ
Stadtarchiv

7. Old Testament. Hs. II/61
Latin. 2 columns. Paper. Folio.
Formerly in the possession of the Capuchin monks in Mainz, given by them to the Augustine monastery, also in Mainz; later in the library of the old university there. Mainz, c. 1455.
Hellmut Lehmann-Haupt, *Gutenberg and the Master of the Playing Cards* (New Haven, Yale University Press, 1966), p. 18, figure 11. According to Dr. Presser, the contemporary binding of Hs. II/61 has the same blind tooling as the B-42 in the Gutenberg Museum, which makes it possible to date the manuscript c. 1455.

The manuscript ends with the Psalter. It contains 18 pages with illuminations, many of their elements comparable to GMB, although in some instances a little coarser. Here and there silver is used instead of gold, the silver having oxidized.

F.8r, the beginning of St. Jerome's Prologues, is of double interest. The page, a portion of which is reproduced in figure 8, contains not only quite lavish borders of acanthus-type foliage and a blossom closely linked with GMB (top borders, figure 13) but also no fewer than five miniatures that correspond with the work of the Master of the Playing Cards: three men from the human suit, a reclining deer, and the "bear sucking its paw."

Some portions of the pages are missing from this manuscript, too (the initial on f.8r has been cut away), but the remaining illuminations show clearly the close connection with GMB, as in the blossom within the initial letter in figure 7. One page has been completely separated from the manuscript and is briefly described below, as No. 8.

Gutenberg Museum

8. Single leaf from the codex listed above as No. 7.
Described in Lehmann-Haupt, *op. cit.*, p. 18. It is illustrated in color in *Gutenberg-Museum der Stadt Mainz* (Munich, Peter Winkler Verlag, 1966). In the background of initial *L* is the deer scratching its head, before a tapestrylike diaper pattern on gold ground. There is also a very fine multicolored border running from the top of the page into the lower margin, painted splendidly according to GMB.

Gutenberg Museum

9. Devotionale ex diversis collectum in unum

Paper.

Lehmann-Haupt, *op. cit.*, p. 27, figure 19.

The manuscript has a number of playing-card motifs and also illuminations after GMB; they are, however, not very closely related. The work is included here for the record only.

Gutenberg Museum. On loan from the Stadtbibliothek.

    10. Missale of the Archbishop D. von Erbach, who gave the codex to the St. Gangolph Stift. The so-called St. Gangolph Missale.

Latin. Thick folio. Vellum.

F.1v, the inscription, *Missale Moguntinum ad usum Collegiatae Ec:clesiae S. Gangolphi mart.* Below, two paragraphs, one headed *Donum*, the other *Fundatio.* On the last but one page, the inscription, *Scriptus [sic] este librer, anno 1444 secundum calendarium.*

    This volume, too, has suffered from the theft of about 50 initials and other decorative features. However, enough illuminations have survived to enable us to say that the St. Gangolph missal is of very high quality and very close to GMB. The layout of the decorations on f.20v, which has fine examples of rather large borders wound around a staff (as in GMB f.11r), has been repeated on 20 subsequent pages. The influence of GMB is evident in the border and terminal blossom in figure 14 and in the border and checkered background of the initial letter in figure 15.

Gutenberg Museum. On loan from the Stadtbibliothek. Hs.II/247.

    11. Devotionale ex diversis collectum in unum. Hs. II/247.

Paper.

Lehmann-Haupt, *op. cit.*, p. 27, note 7, figure 19.

A late ownership entry: "Iste liber precarius donatus est Bibliothecae Conventus Mogentini ord. FF. Erem. S. S. Augustini 1744."

    This manuscript appears also to be of Mainz origin, although its provenance is not absolutely certain.

    The quality of the workmanship is very low, at times even dilettante. Some of the miniatures show relationship to the engraved playing cards. However, the over-all impression of the illuminations is that they may be copies from another manuscript rather than direct examples of the GMB's instructions.

Dom Museum

    12A to F. Six Carmelite choir books

4. See Fritz Arens, *Die Kunstdenkmäler der Stadt Mainz* (*Kunstdenkmäler von Rheinland-Pfalz*. Bd. 4), Part I, "Kirchen St. Agnes bis Hl. Kreuz" (München-Berlin, Deutscher Kunstverlag, 1961), pp. 455–95. Discusses also some of the most important illuminations.

5. Discussed by Arens, *op. cit.*

Large, thick folios, with sizable musical notation, richly illustrated and decorated. Made for the Carmelite Monastery and Church.[4]
This is a monumental set. The six volumes were originally produced to be placed on lecterns for the choir's use during services.
Mainz, second quarter of the fifteenth century.
The volumes have no call or shelf marks, so they were assigned Roman capitals from A to F to distinguish them from each other.

The large size of the leaves of these choir books presented a special problem to the illuminators, which they met very successfully. Many of the acanthus leaves were obviously made from study of GMB, but a number of the initials and borders are in a style quite different from GMB. Others are reminiscent of GMB, but with enough differences to recognize that the connections in these cases are not direct. Clearly, a detailed listing of illuminations, although it concentrated only upon the GMB connections, would be too long and tedious to read.

12A. In order to fill the margins with appropriate ornamentation, the large foliage wrapped around a staff, as on f.11v of GMB, was frequently used in this as well as in the other volumes. On several pages we find close connections with GMB, but quite often blended skillfully with initials, calligraphic ornamentations, etc. that were not derived from GMB. F.48v has a border of finely executed leaves wound around a staff and an initial background described and painted in GMB on f.8r.

F.60r has an exquisite initial *R*, calligraphic decorations executed with high skill, and some leafy borders reminiscent of GMB without following it too closely. This successful pattern is repeated many times: on 72r, 80r, 112r, 122v, 127v, 137v, 142r, 149r, 173v, 187v, and 209r.

12B. This codex has a large dedication page, not connected with GMB.[5] An initial *E* on f.1r reminds one strongly of the famous initial *B* in the Fust and Schöffer Psalter of 1457. Along with many "classic" GMB motifs, the codex contains much independently designed illumination, for instance, the large historiated miniature on f.242v. Influence of GMB appears in the treatment of the acanthus leaf in the borders of the page shown in figure 16 as well as in the upright members of the initial letter, which is ornamented with the checkered background of GMB.

12C. Here, too, is a mixture of GMB elements, closely integrated with illuminations that are merely reminiscent of the Model Book, executed by quite different hands from another atelier. In this latter group belongs the large historiated initial on f.1r, f.66r (Christ's Ascension), closely related to f.1r, and a very rich initial *I*.

12D. On f.4r is the largest foliage border, winding around a staff (GMB 11r), that appears in these works, but it is necessary to add that the quality of the illumination here is not of the first order.

12E. In this volume are some exquisite large illuminations not directly connected with GMB, namely, f.278r, 279v, 312r, and 385v. The layout and execution noted under 12A, f.60r, is followed here in E, on f.321v, 332r, 340v, 356r, 365v, 371r, 379v, and 382v.

It should be understood that among the "classic" GMB-type illuminations are some that have been adapted to the format of these volumes by using larger sizes of leafy scrolls or by elongating them through lateral condensation.

12F. The rich decoration of this volume is only indirectly connected with GMB. The large historiated initials and other miniatures are by different hands. They are found, for instance, on f.1r: the large illuminated initial *A*, ornaments and lettering on all four margins, at the bottom the donors—man and wife—and coat of arms; f.38v: historiated initial with Nativity, the scrollwork only indirectly connected with GMB models; on other leaves the Adoration of the Magi, a Resurrection, and a Pentecost. There are also calligraphic initials that look very much like the scrollwork in the 1457 Psalter.

On f.451v: "Incipit sanctorale scd'm ordinacīm S. Eccl'ie Jh'osolomitare ordinis fratrū beate dei genetricis Marie v'gīs de mōte Carmeli." (Translation: "Here begins the book of saints' lives according to the arrangement of the Holy Church of Jerusalem of the order of the brothers of the Blessed Mother of God, the Virgin Mary of Mt. Carmel.")

On f.485v a large initial historiated with a group of Carmelite brothers singing from a large choir book, a direct illustration of the use of these six volumes.

PARIS
Bibliothèque Nationale

13. The 42-line Bible
4 volumes. Vellum.
Mainz, Johann Gutenberg, before 1454.
B-42, Velins 67–70.
Seymour De Ricci, *Catalogue Raisonné des Premièrs Impressions de Mayence*, No. 11; Paul Schwenke, *Ergänzungsband*, 23; Edward Lazare, *The Gutenberg Bible: A Census* (Newark, N.J., 1956), No. 3; Don Cleveland Norman, *Pictorial Census of the Gutenberg Bible* (Chicago, Coverdale Press, 1961), No. 21 with illustrations, figures 111–114.

Like those made for the Gutenberg Bible in Göttingen, these bindings, too, are surpassingly beautiful. They are of royal red morocco and bear the gilt arms of Louis XV; the arrangement of the sizes of decorations is graded to the importance of the passage each precedes.

The four volumes are specially attractive in that no initials or borders have been excised. The top margins and the outer edges of the leaves have been somewhat trimmed, without noticeable damage to text or decoration. Characteristic for this set is the use of silver in the initials, which in several cases has not oxidized and which never occurs in GMB. In Volume I, at the *Prologues in pentateucum* there is an initial *D*, the decoration of which can be seen again and again in the other volumes. These initials are generally related to GMB. Their backgrounds are usually built up from GMB's acanthus leaves and blossoms in ever-different combinations.

The next large initial in Volume I is the splendid initial *I* (*Incipit Genesis*), with borders developed from the GMB blossom and occasionally combined with GMB leafy scrollwork. The stems of this and other initials are derived from GMB f.10v. This and other initials are beautifully developed from GMB, but with some originality in the composition, as in figures 9 and 10. A number of initials in this set are independent of GMB.

It must be stated that the quality of illumination varies a good deal in these four volumes. A really detailed analysis, with characterization of the various elements, would be possible only if this set could be compared with GMB and other volumes influenced by it. It would be most interesting to assemble all these codices in one place and compare them at first hand.

WASHINGTON
Library of Congress
14. The Giant Bible of Mainz
2 volumes. Vellum.[6]

One of the unexplained and puzzling questions aroused by this wonderful manuscript is the abrupt interruption of the illumination after f.31 of the first volume. The scribes' work was completed, according to the date entered in the Giant Bible, on July 9, 1453. Throughout the two volumes one finds, here and there, outline drawings for miniatures that remain incomplete. Strangely, the last 9 pages of Volume II are embellished with perfectly executed initials in full color. Of special interest for us is the initial *A* on f.210v, at the beginning of St. John's *Apocalypse*. The background of this initial (figure 17) is executed exactly according to the first background in the Model Book (f.8r). It is a very polished and accomplished performance, but it is not

6. Dorothy Miner, *The Giant Bible of Mainz, 500th Anniversary* (Washington, D.C., 1952); Hellmut Lehmann-Haupt, *Gutenberg and the Master of the Playing Cards* (New Haven, Yale University Press, 1966), many references.

by the Master of GMB or a member of his atelier. It would be very difficult to describe the differences, but someone who has studied the Model Book and the many illuminations made according to its instructions will recognize the differences at once. By the way, only the background of this initial *A* corresponds to GMB; the fillings of the letter and the marginal scrolls are not related. The appearance of this single example of a GMB initial among a series of other initials in the last signature of the Giant Bible is genuinely mystifying.

WHAT PRICE ILLUMINATION

The Butzbach Bible in the Giessen University Library (see page 83) is certainly not more than a pathetic ruin, as indicated in the catalog description, but its remnants afford features of unique interest. On the inside of the back cover, which is lined with vellum, there are two inscriptions (figure 11) in the same hand; one is near the top edge and of very great interest,[7] the other is one of four incomplete lines near the bottom and not so interesting. The top inscription reads,[8] "Perfectum est hoc opus biblie decimanona mensis septembris constatque scriptura 12 [?] florenos 16 solidos heleros / Illuminatura $2\frac{1}{2}$ florenos / bapirus 2 florenos / ligatura 1 florenum / summa 24 florenos 2 solidos."

Translated, this inscription reads:
"This work of the Bible was completed on the 19th of the month of September and the price of the writing was 12 [?] guilders 16 shillings; of the illumination $2\frac{1}{2}$ guilders; of the paper 2 guilders; the binding 1 guilder; the sum total 24 guilders and 2 shillings."

The relationship of these figures to present-day currency would require the expertise of a specialist in middle Rhenish currency of the mid-fifteenth century in order to enlighten us on the purchasing power of the sums mentioned. Such a study would be very worth while, since the itemized costs of book production of the time would constitute a document of great value. Obviously, the writing of the text, as might be expected, is the largest item on the list (even if the questioned 12 should be read as another, probably higher, figure). By comparison, the illumination, at $2\frac{1}{2}$ guilders, was a relatively modest cost—only half a guilder more than the paper. The binding, 1 guilder, was the lowest item on the list. Added to the uncertainties about medieval money values is the question of how the specified sums could add up to 24 guilders and 2 shillings. Pursuing the matter of the cost of these beautiful books is

7. See Lehmann-Haupt, *op. cit.*, p. 63.
8. I consulted Dr. Joachim Kirchner on the correct reading of these inscriptions, who in turn consulted Prof. Werner Bischoff.

9. In his definitive *Johannes Gutenberg, sein Leben und sein Werk* (Berlin, Mann, 1947; 3d ed., Nieuwkoop, 1967).

Aloys Ruppel's mention of the Giessen manuscript and the compensation paid the scribe.[9] He estimates that the writing of the Bible must have taken one-and-a-fourth to one-and-a-half years; from the known costs of the book, it would seem that the scribe earned, annually, not quite 10 guilders. He also tells us that in Strassburg in 1450 a Bible written on parchment cost 60 guilders; the Gotha copy of the *Catholicon*, printed on paper in Mainz in 1460, cost 41 guilders, including rubrication and binding.

The inscription at the bottom of the back cover of the Butzbach Bible deals with private reading notes made by the first owner of the Bible, as follows:
"Item duplicavi horam tribus annis Item incepi legere in biblia anno domini 1454. In die beatorum symonis et iude apostolorum / Item neglexi 8 ebdomades Item duas / Item incepi legere nocturnam Anno LX octauo nativitatis in die / Item cessavi Anno 63 Symonis et jude."

Translated, this inscription reads:
"I did the canonical hours twice for three years. Then I began to read in the Bible in the year of our Lord 1454 on the day of the blessed Simon and Jude the apostles. I failed to do this once for eight weeks, at another time for two weeks. Then I began to read the book of night services in the year 1460 on the eighth day of Christmas. This I stopped doing on the feast of Simon and Jude in the year 1463."

One important fact is clear from these notes: The manuscript was completed by the year 1454, and certainly by September 19 of that year.

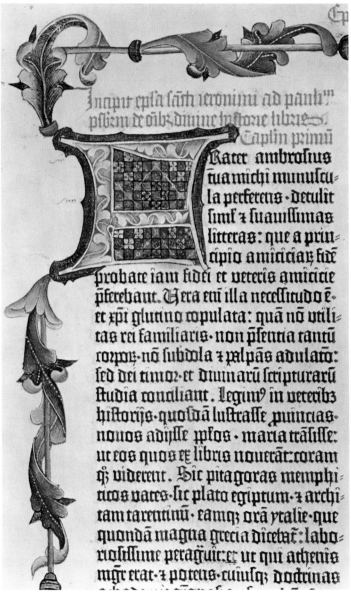

Figure 1. Göttingen Gutenberg Bible. Beginning of f.1r.

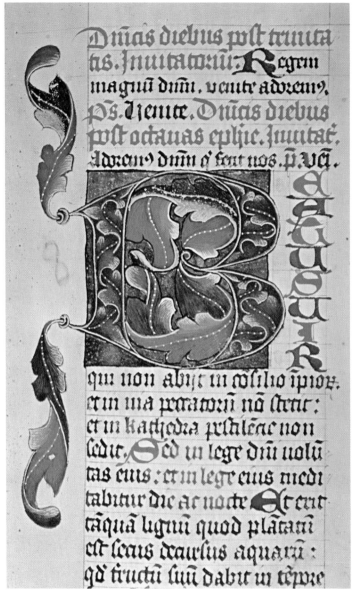

Figure 2. Frankfurt a. M., University Library. MS. Barth. 40. Portion of f.29r.

Figure 3. Frankfurt a. M., University Library.
MS. Barth. 158. Portion of f.27r.

Figure 4. Frankfurt a. M., University Library.
MS. Barth. 158. Portion of f.67v.

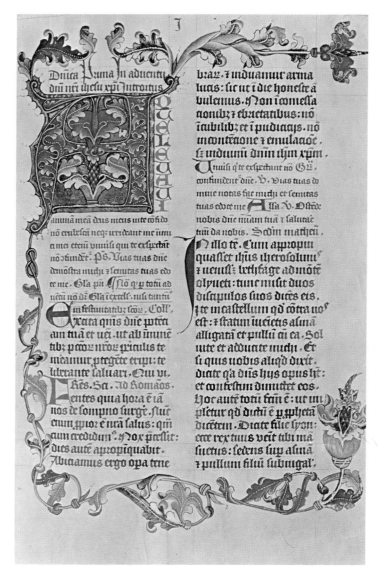

Figure 5. Frankfurt a. M., University Library.
MS. Barth. 31. f.1r.

Figure 6. Frankfurt a. M., University Library.
MS. Barth. 31. Portion of f.10v.

Figure 7. Mainz, Municipal Archives.
Hs. II/61. Portion of f.49v.

Figure 8. Mainz, Municipal Archives.
Hs. II/61. Portion of f.8r.

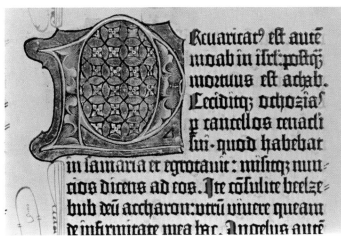

Figure 9. Paris, Bibliothèque Nationale. Gutenberg
Bible, Velins 68. Beginning of Liber Regum quartus.

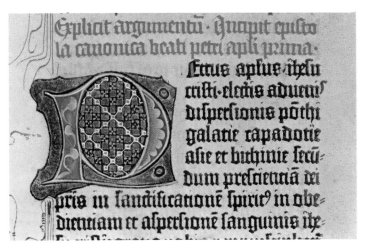

Figure 10. Paris, Bibliothèque Nationale. Gutenberg
Bible, Velins 70. Beginning of Epist. canonica B. Petri.

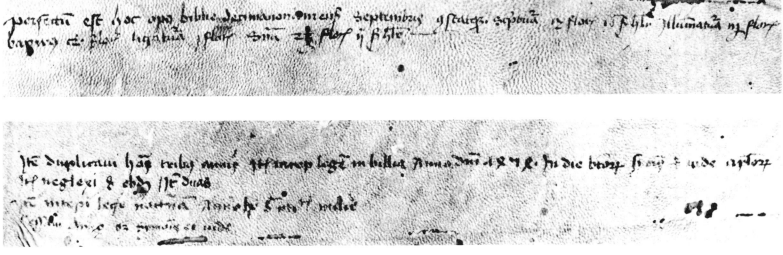

Figure 11. Giessen, University Library. Butzbach Bible. The two ms. entries on the inside of the back cover.

Figure 12. Giessen, University Library. Butzbach Bible. Portion of a page with initial letter E.

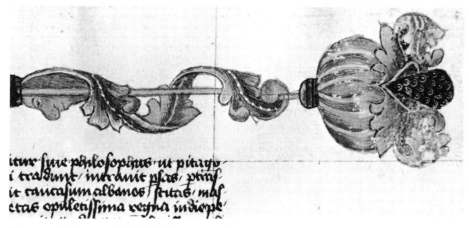

Figure 13. Mainz, Municipal Archives. Hs. II/61. Upper right corner of f.8r.

Figure 14. Mainz, Gutenberg Museum, loan from the Municipal Library. The St. Gangolph's Missal. Hs. II/136. Portion of f.135v.

Figure 15. Mainz, Gutenberg Museum, loan from the Municipal Library. The St. Gangolph's Missal. Hs. II/136. Portion of f.135v.

Figure 16. Mainz, Dom Museum.
Carmelite Choir Book, MS. B.

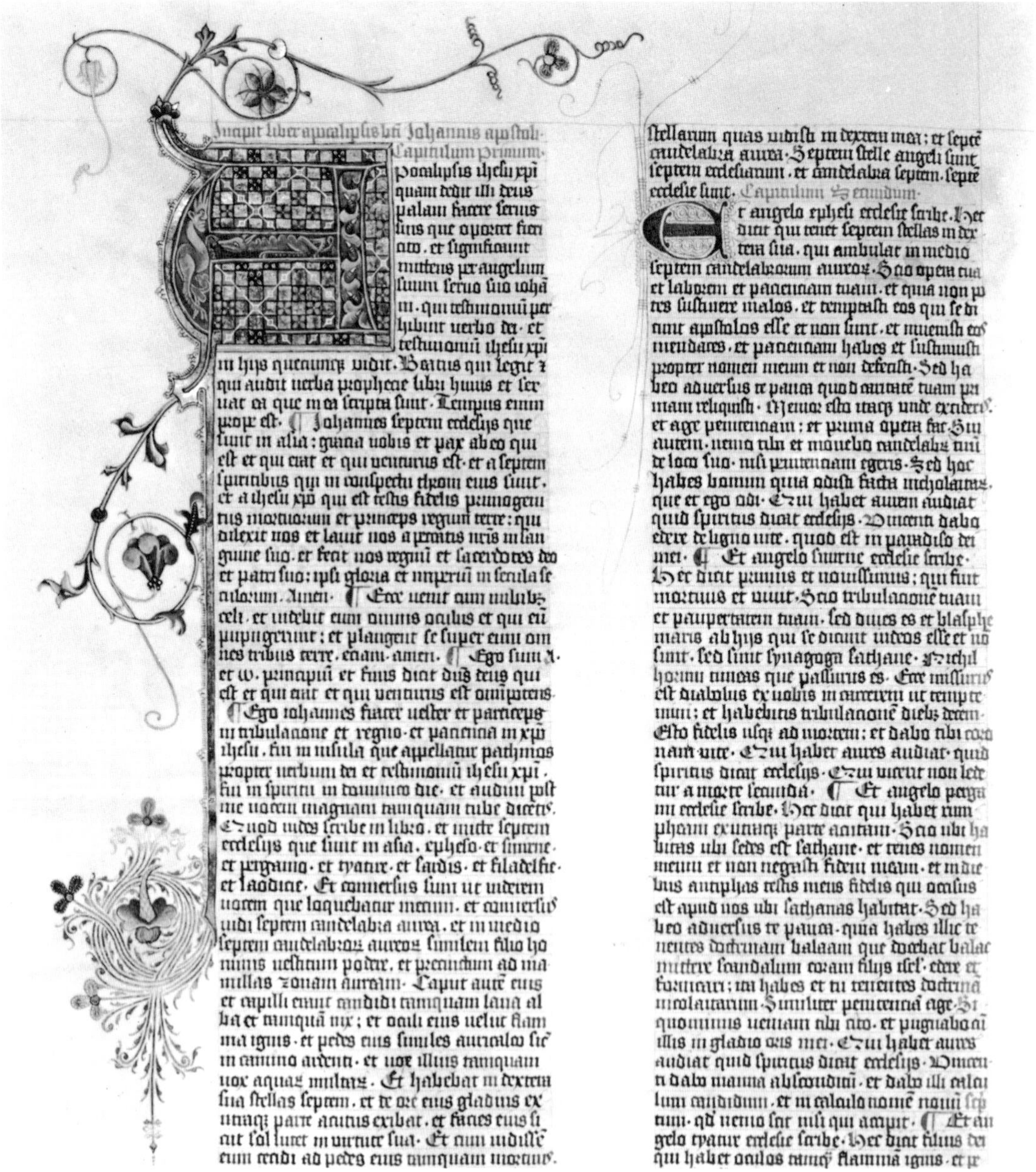

Figure 17. Washington, D.C., Library of Congress. The Giant Bible of Mainz, Vol. II. Portion of f.210v.

One question should be discussed here. It concerns the attribution of GMB to Mainz and its probable date. Dr. Joachim Kirchner, the world's leading expert on German Gothic paleography, examined the handwriting of GMB in the summer of 1969 in my presence and declared it to be a good, typical example of Frankish Bastarda, a practical book hand with strong cursive admixtures. The late Dr. Edmund Will was of the opinion (in a letter addressed to Prof. Dr. A. Bruckner, Reinach near Basel) that the lower portions of f.5r and the first 14 lines of f.5v were written by a different scribe. These lines do seem slightly different, and they were perhaps written by another hand. It does not seem to me that the evidence is fully conclusive, however. The scribe may have been interrupted, a different mixture of ink may have been used, or some other unknown circumstances may have caused the slight differences.

As for the evidence of the language used in GMB, Dr. Will has "characterized its dialect as Rhenish Franconian with traces of Alemanic, which points to an origin in Mainz or somewhat south of that city."[1]

GMB, as has been stated earlier, is not dated, but the evidence to be gathered from the volumes that were illuminated according to its instructions is conclusive. The two Gutenberg Bibles, one in Göttingen, the other in the Bibliothèque Nationale in Paris, furnish hard evidence. Aloys Ruppel states,[2] "We may conclude, with a measure of probability, that Gutenberg produced his printing apparatus between 1450 and 1452 and that composition and presswork of the 42-line Bible was begun in 1452." He also writes, "The printing of the 42-line Bible was completed by the middle of 1455 at the latest." The *Gesamtkatalog der Wiegendrucke* (GW 4201) places the completion of printing c. 1454–1455. The date 1454 in the Butzbach Bible in Giessen fits in neatly with this chronology. There is no reason to assume that GMB and its workshop functioned for only a few years. Its activities may well have extended ten, twenty, even thirty years before and after the middle of the century.

With the exception of the Carmelite choir book F, none of the manuscripts dependent on GMB seem to contain a specific notation of their Mainz origin. But where else could they have been illuminated? It is reasonable to assume that the illuminator's workshop that used GMB remained in Mainz and did not migrate from place to place. To transport to another city the large and thick Carmelite choir books, for instance, would have been awkward and, perhaps, hazardous for their preservation. The illumination of the two Gutenberg Bibles that are now in Göttingen and in Paris does not add to the evidence of their being produced in Mainz, since Gutenberg Bibles are known to have been illuminated outside of Mainz. At best, these two well-identified books can be considered only as collateral evidence of illumination in a Mainz atelier. In sum, there is no reason to assume that GMB and the volumes

1. Hellmut Lehmann-Haupt, *Gutenberg and the Master of the Playing Cards* (New Haven, Yale University Press, 1966), p. 21.

2. Aloys Ruppel, *Johannes Gutenberg, sein Leben und sein Werk* (Berlin, Mann, 1947; 3d ed., Nieuwkoop, 1967). My translation.

illuminated according to its instruction were produced elsewhere than Mainz; no evidence points away from Mainz. The volumes in the Frankfurt Library were attributed to Frankfurt by Swarzenski and Schilling on the basis of their provenance. But it is not at all difficult to point out that they could very well have been illuminated in nearby Mainz rather than in Frankfurt.

There is one question I would like to raise before concluding. Are the Göttingen and Berlin model books fragments? Were they once part of what I have designated elsewhere as the "hypothetical Mainz Modelbook," the one used by the Master of the Playing Cards, the illuminator of the Giant Bible of Mainz, the Scheide Gutenberg Bible, etc.? There is some evidence pointing in this direction, such as the casual beginning and end of the two model books, the reference to flowers and miniatures on folio 6v of GMB, and the fact that some Mainz manuscripts contain both motifs and figures from the model books corresponding to the engraved playing cards. In a very thorough and detailed review of the GMB in *Speculum*, vol. 49, no. 2, Professor Harry Bober is strongly of the opinion that it is the surviving part of a larger, more comprehensive model book. I also asked Professor Anzelewski whether the existence of the two model books could be thought to strengthen theories about the existence of a larger model book. He answered (my translation):

> The question . . . has to be answered in the affirmative; since our (the Berlin) manuscript contains apparently more text than the Göttingen. Since beyond that there existed an upper-Rhenish manuscript that was larger, it is to be assumed that our two manuscripts were excerpts from it or a fourth one.

The upper-Rhenish manuscript referred to here is related in its dialect to the Göttingen and Berlin model books. It was published as *Quellen und Technik der Fresko-, Oel-, und Tempera-Malerei des Mittelalters, von der byzantischen Zeit bis einschliesslich der "Erfindung der Ölmalerei" durch die Brüder Van Eyck*, by Ernst Berger (Munich, G. D. W. Callway, 1912; reprinted, 1973 by Dr. Martin Sendig O. H. G., Walluf b. Wiesbaden 6229).

We have come to the end of this discussion of the Göttingen Model Book, which I consider only the first of many necessary studies of the book and its influence on fifteenth-century book art. The work projected by Dr. Will would have opened many avenues of research by scholars in the field, and I have taken the initial steps in order to stimulate these further studies and investigations. Close study of both model books, as can be seen from examination of the reproductions in this publication, will be infinitely rewarding to any scholar who undertakes research of one of their many aspects. I look forward with eagerness to their publications.

Library of Congress Cataloging in Publication Data
Göttingen.   Niedersächsische Staats- und Universitäts-
   bibliothek.   MSS.   (Cod. Ms./Uffenb. 51)
   The Göttingen Model Book.

   English or German.
   1.   Illumination of books and manuscripts, Gothic—
Germany—Handbooks, manuals, etc.   2.   Illumination of
books and manuscripts, German—Handbooks, manuals, etc.
I.   Lehmann-Haupt, Hellmut, 1903–   II.   Will, Edmund,
1884–   III.   Title.
ND2980.G6   1978   745.6′7′028   78–62289
ISBN 0–8262–0261–6